Be My Valentine!
Adult Coloring Book
60 Drawings and Patterns To Color

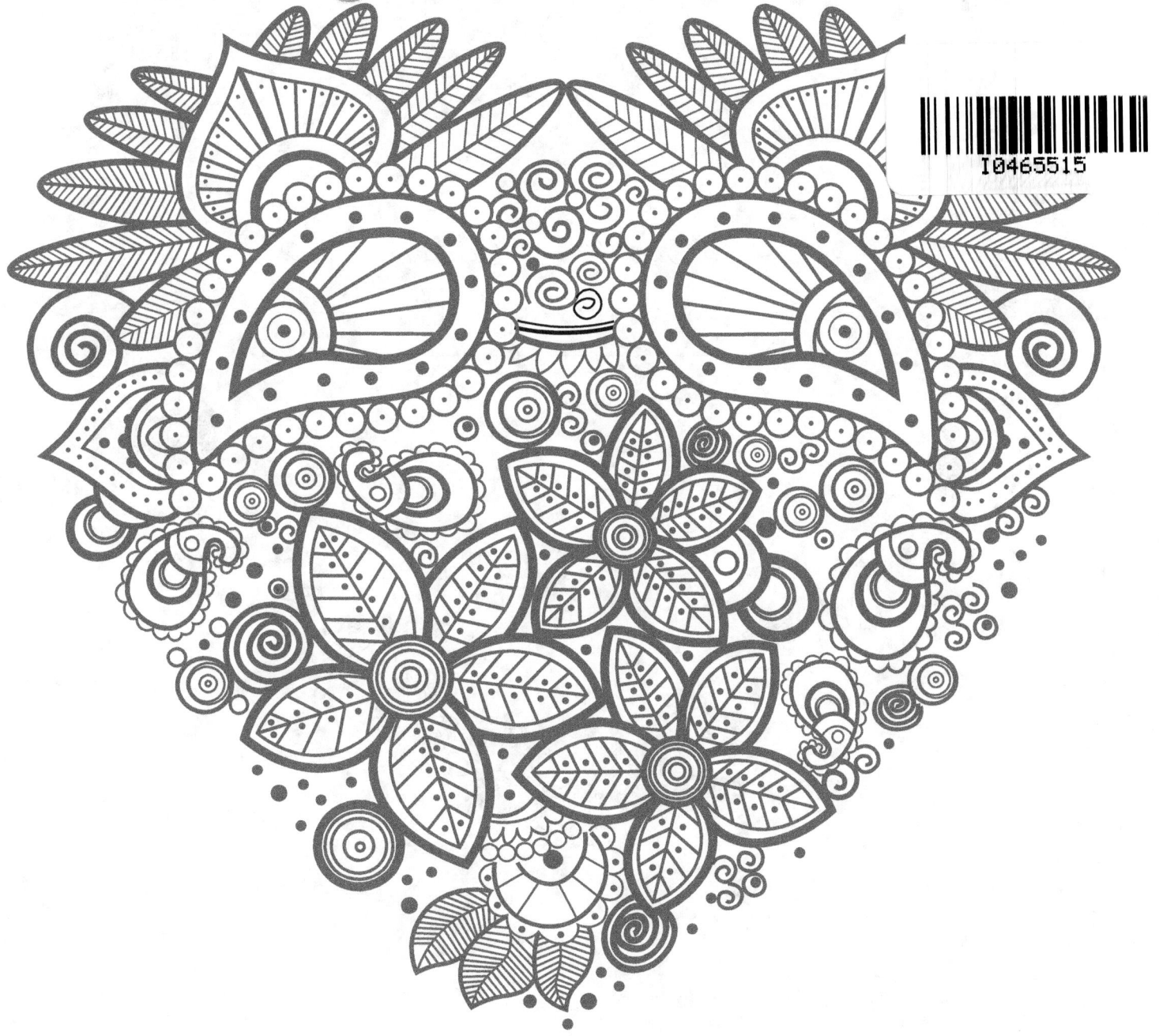

Gholamreza Zare & Pegah Malekpour Alamdari

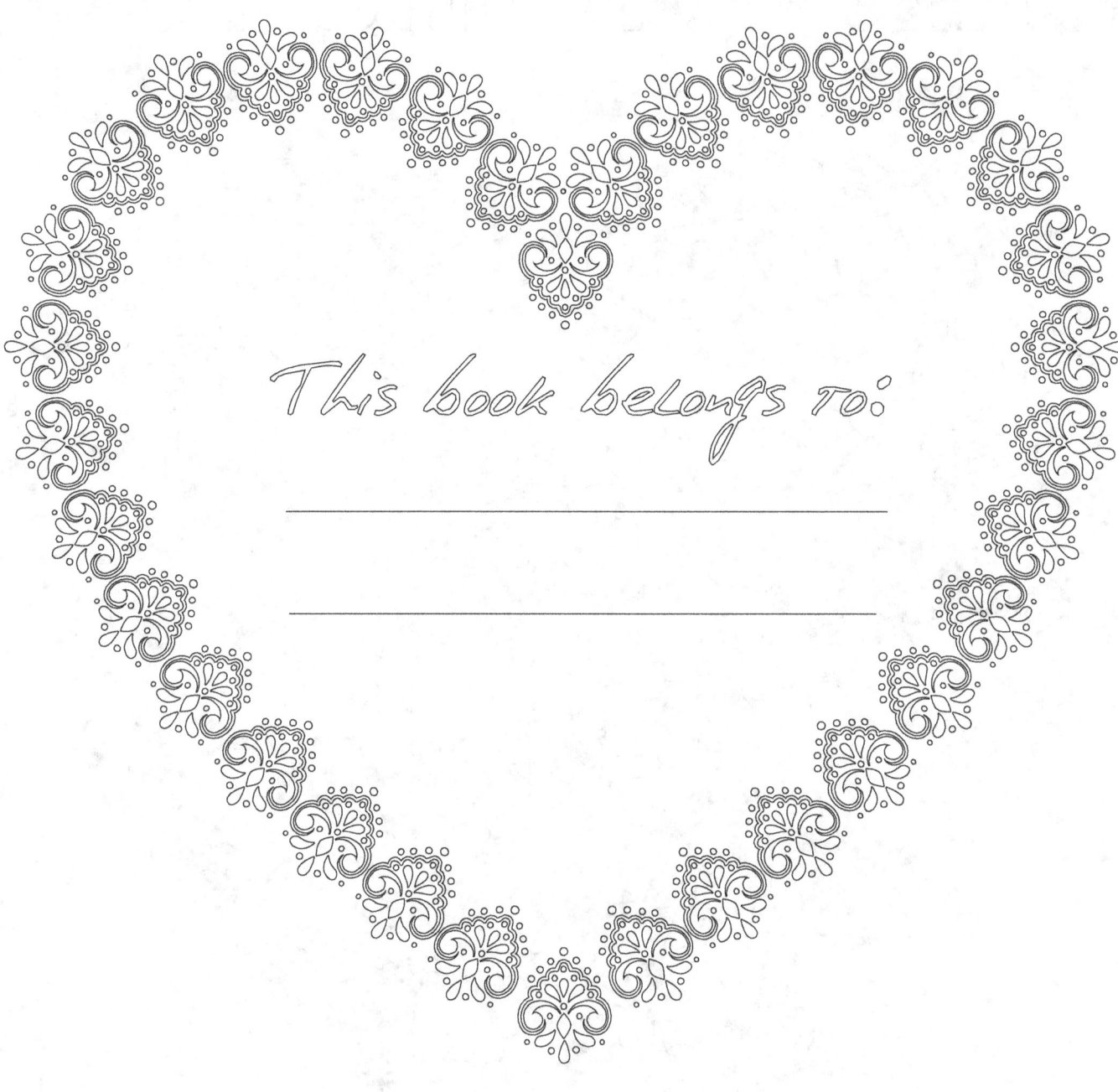

This book belongs to:

_____

_____

Inroduction

We have designed the 60 beautiful, romantic, coloring pages with high resolution to color with the ones you love and also to improve your relaxation time. These heart-themed designs signify your love for your lovely partner. We sure you can present your love precisely by offering the book to him or her that exists in your heart. Your sweet words are behind the drawings of the book. Also, celebrate Valentine's Day by coloring the patterns as you like.

Moreover, there are sufficient spaces around the heart-them designs to write what you like. This book contains the beautiful patterns of flowers, mandalas, heart, geometric, and symmetric design with some lovely messages such as "I Love You.", "Be My Valentine!", "Happy Valentine's Day!" , and "Love". The love message behind the designs makes this book different from other adult coloring book or coloring book for grown-ups.

Also, the designs and illustrations are useful for relaxation and stress relief especially for inspiring romance in your life. We sure you love the book and can see the potential for some great art. The book is great for Valentine's day or anytime as love is timeless. Also, adult coloring books have some advantages to use in meditative activities such as mind relaxation including creativity.

Gholamreza Zare (Ghrzarea@gmail.com)
Pegah Malekpour Alamdari (PegahMalekpour@gmail.com)

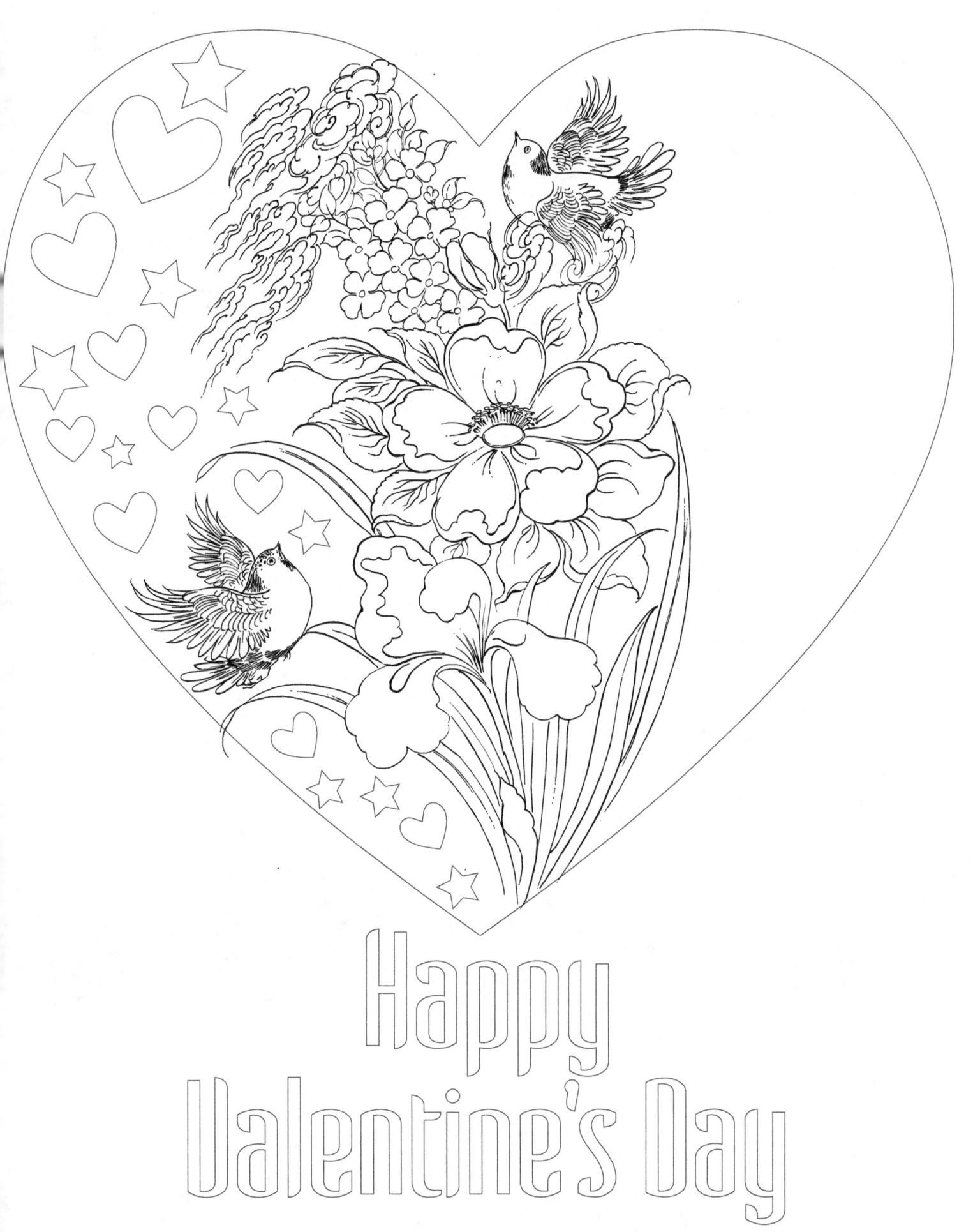

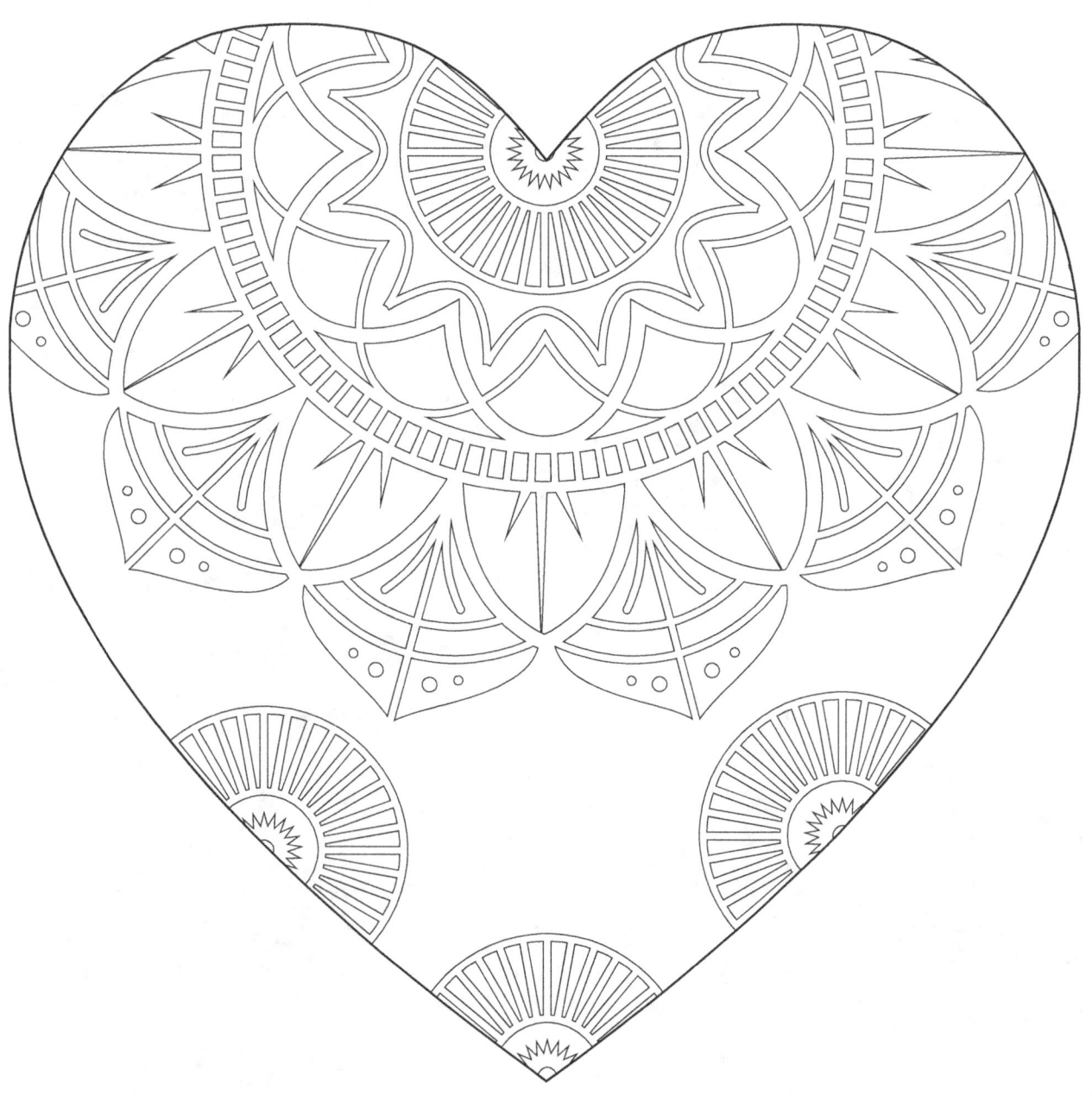

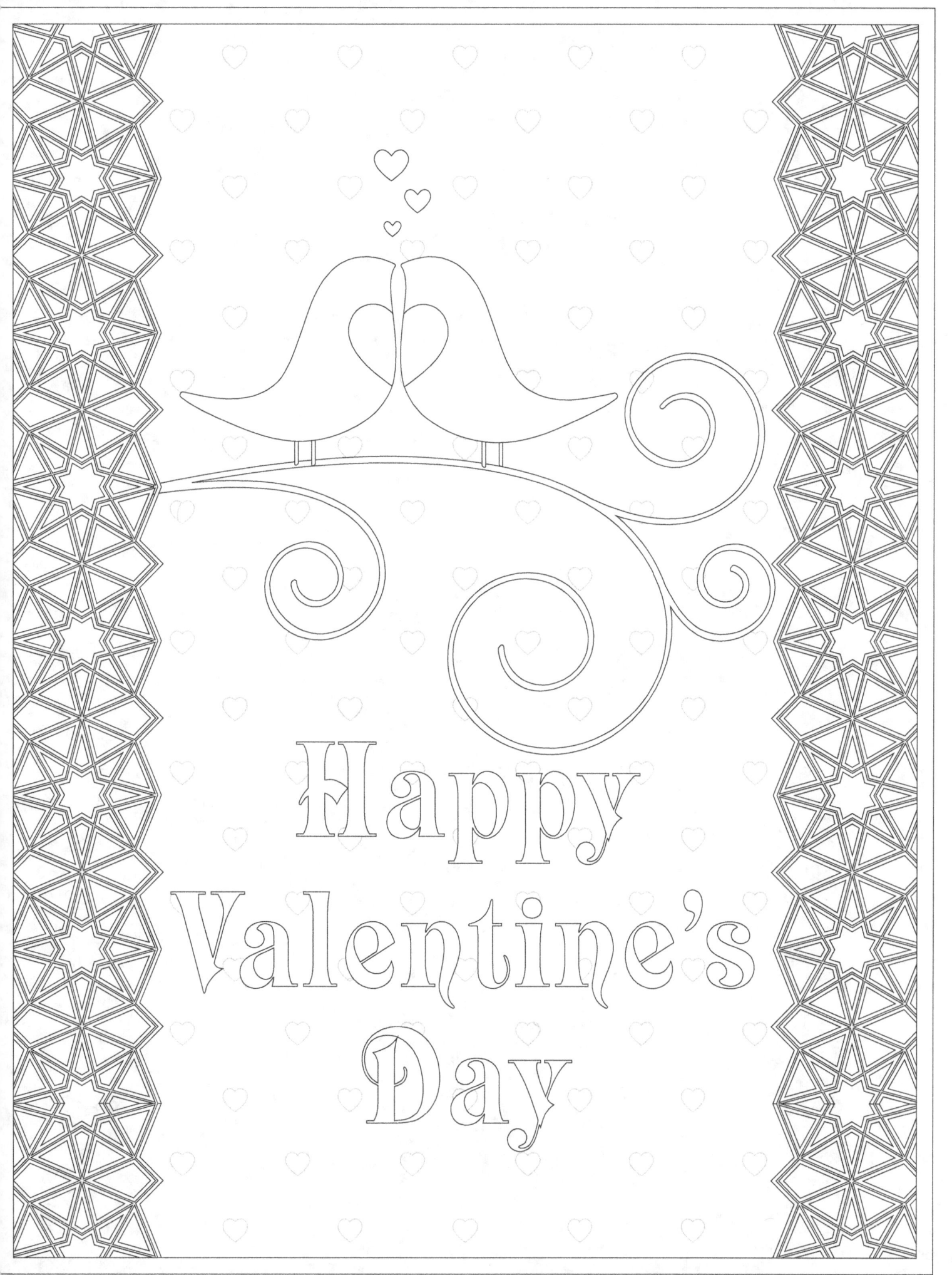

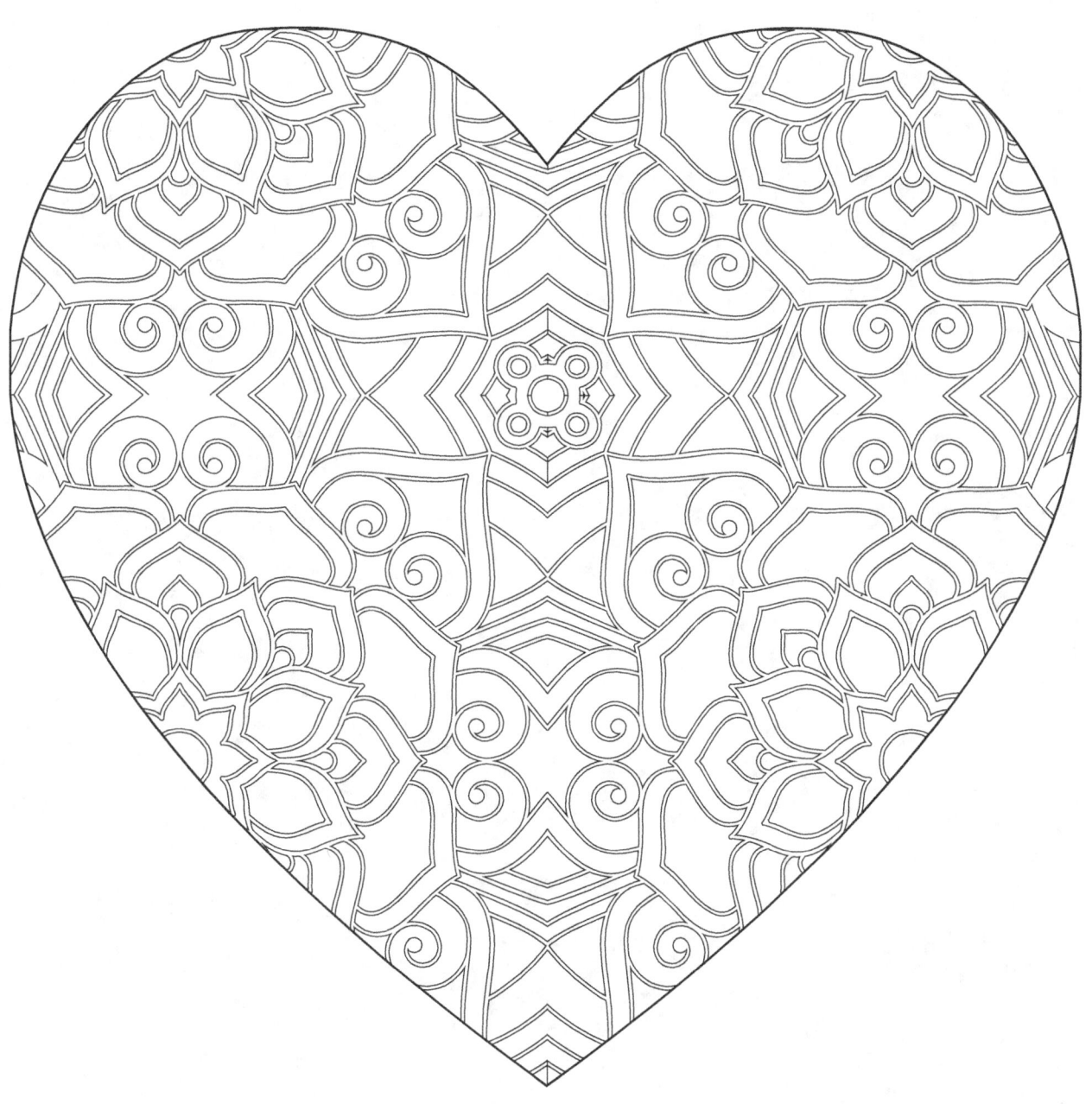

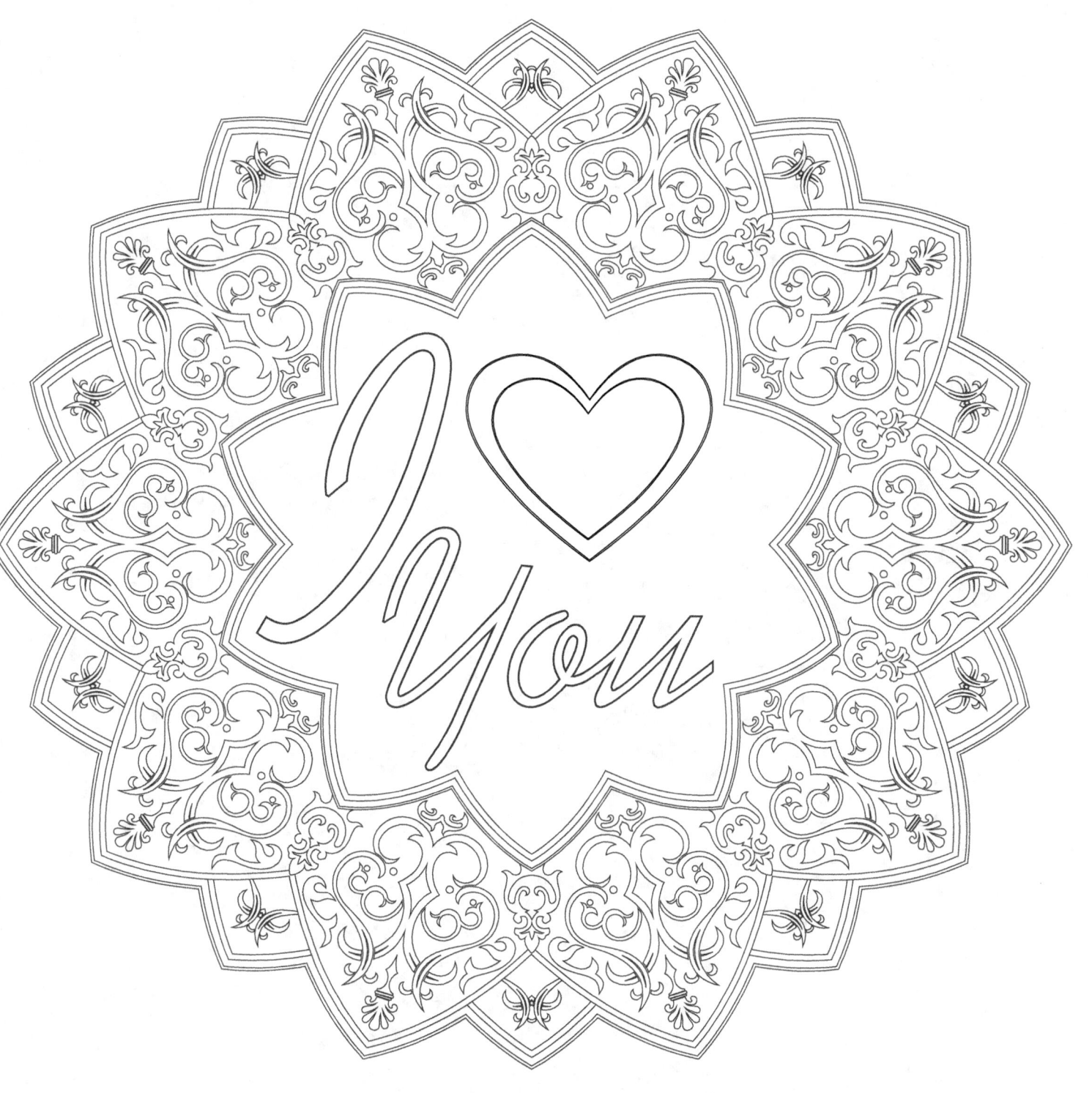

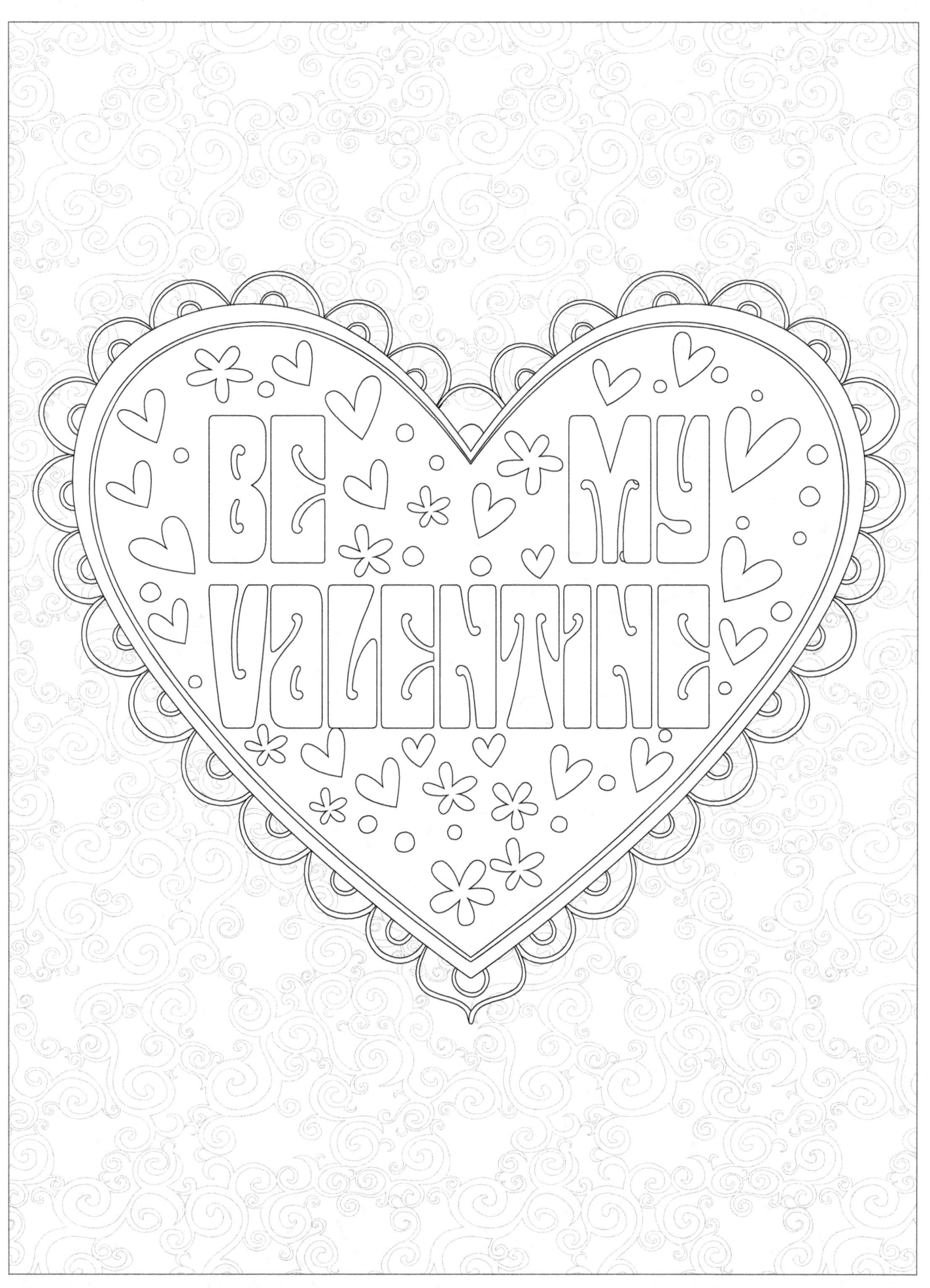

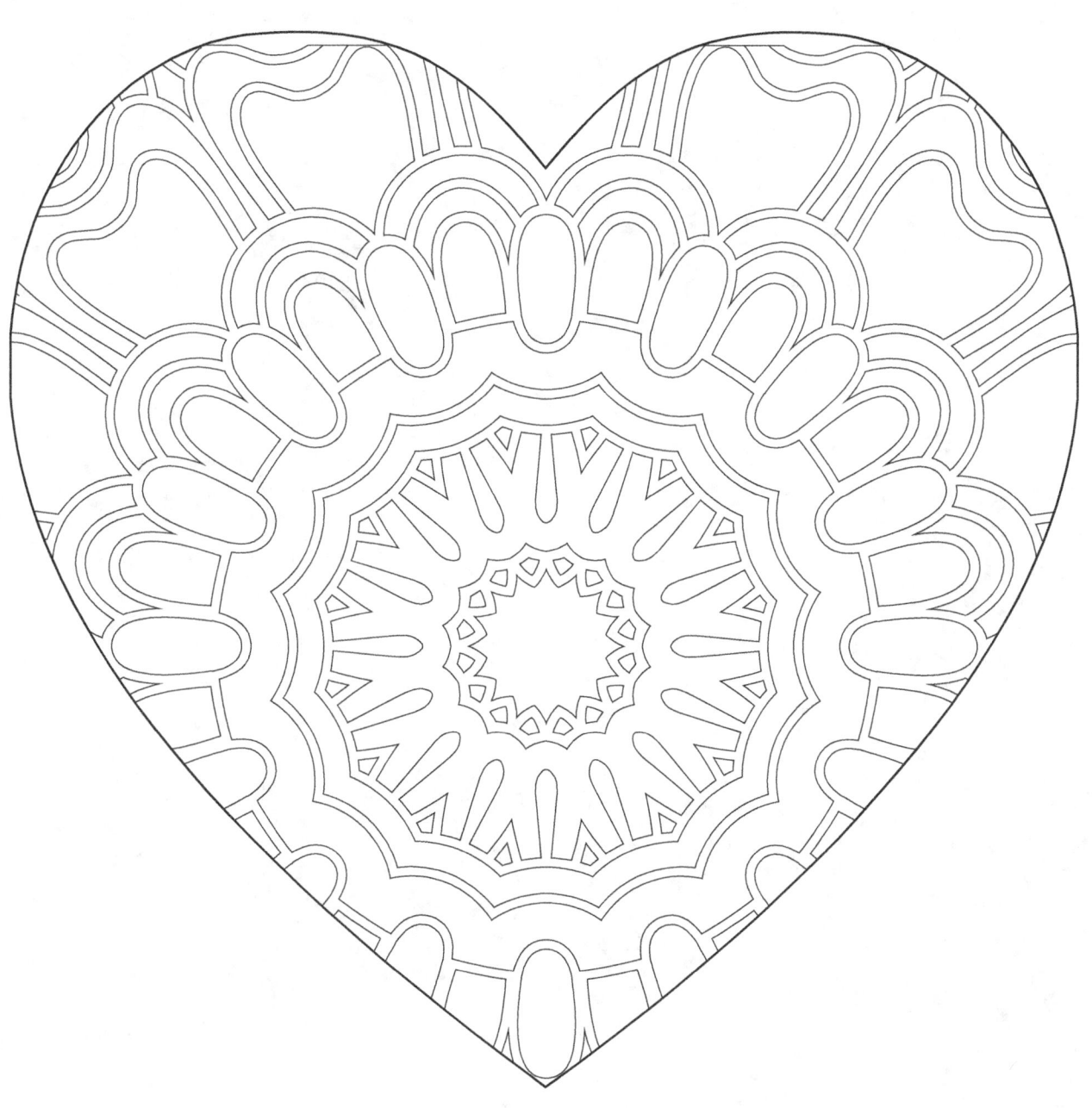

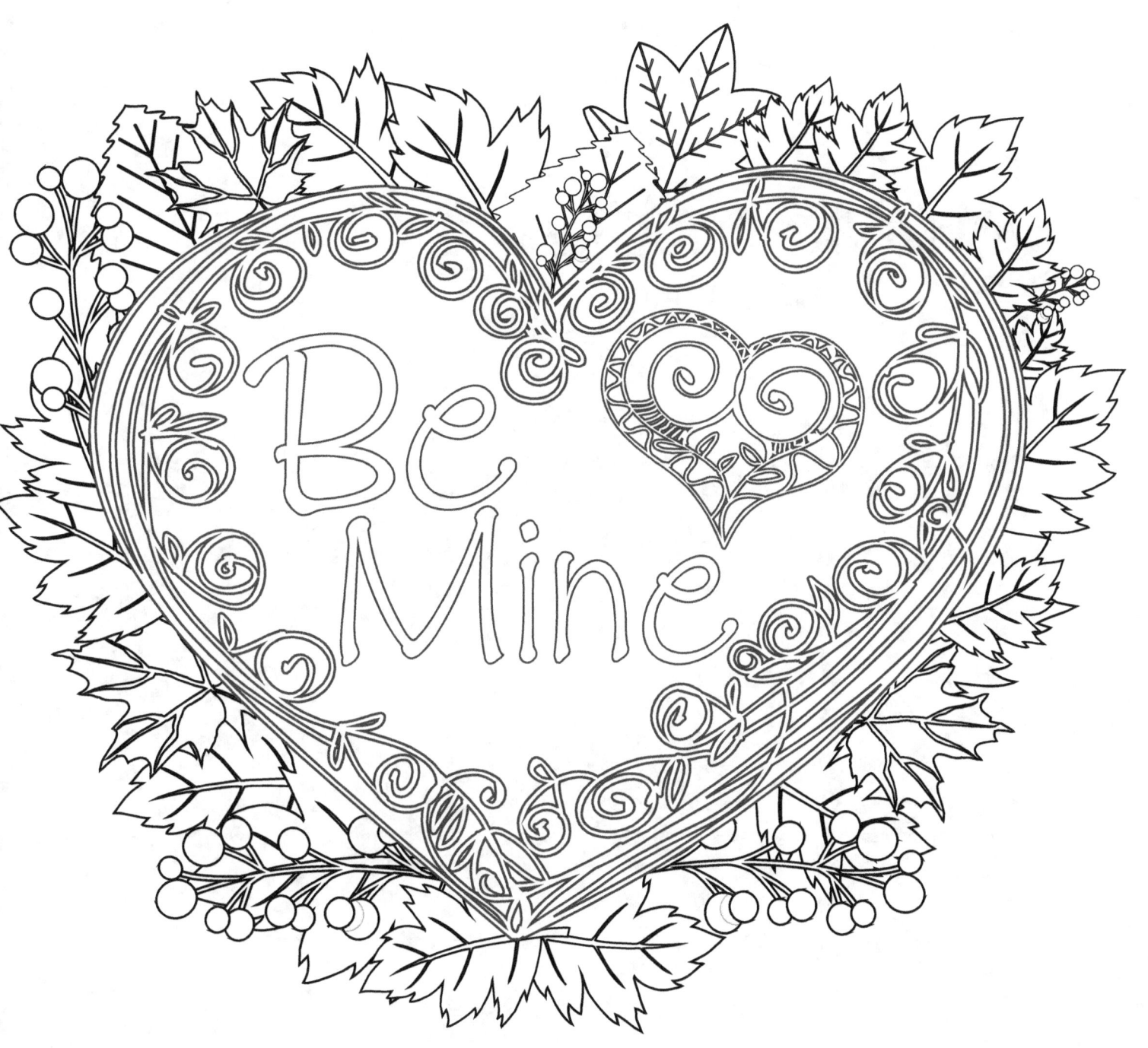

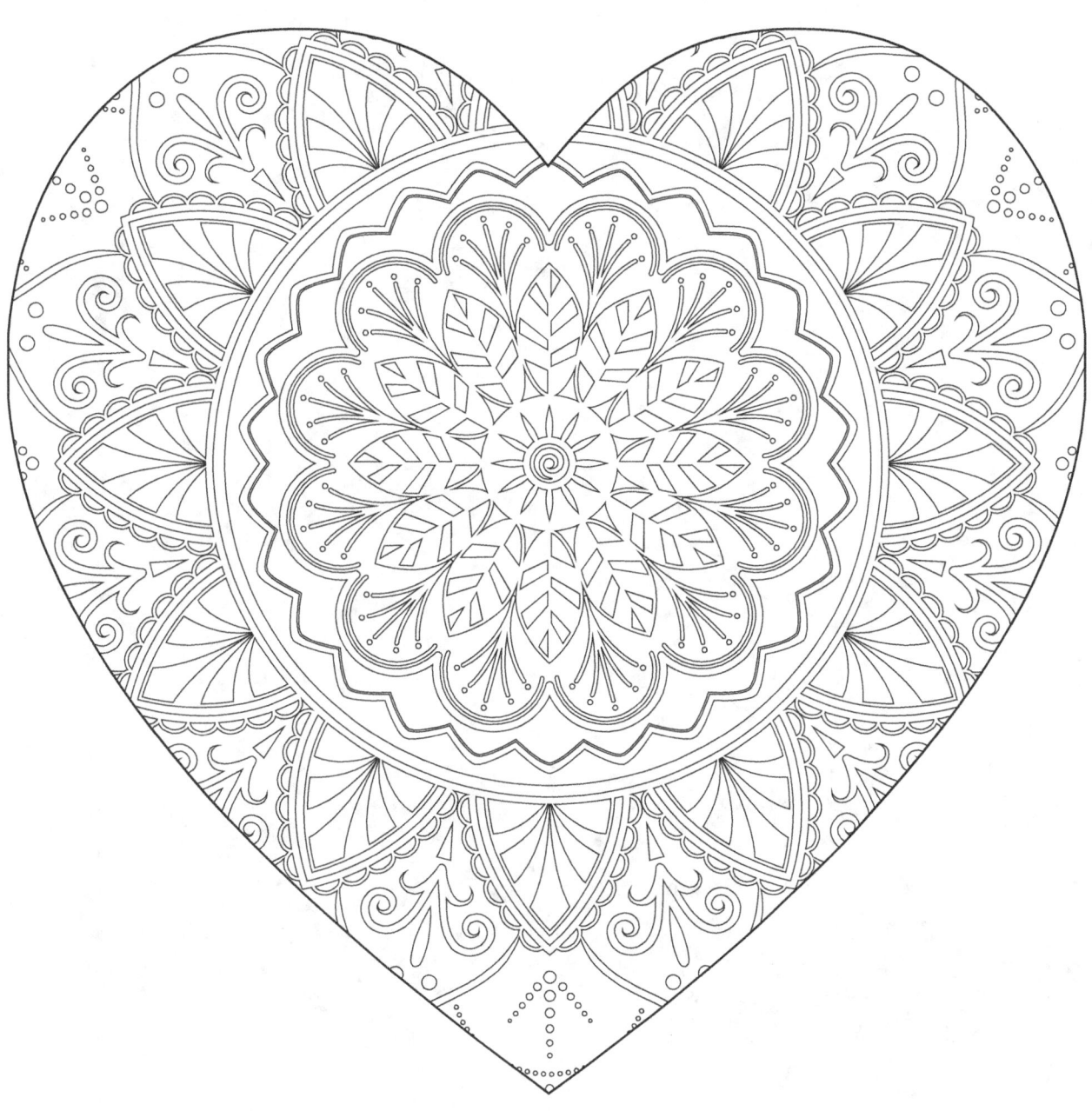

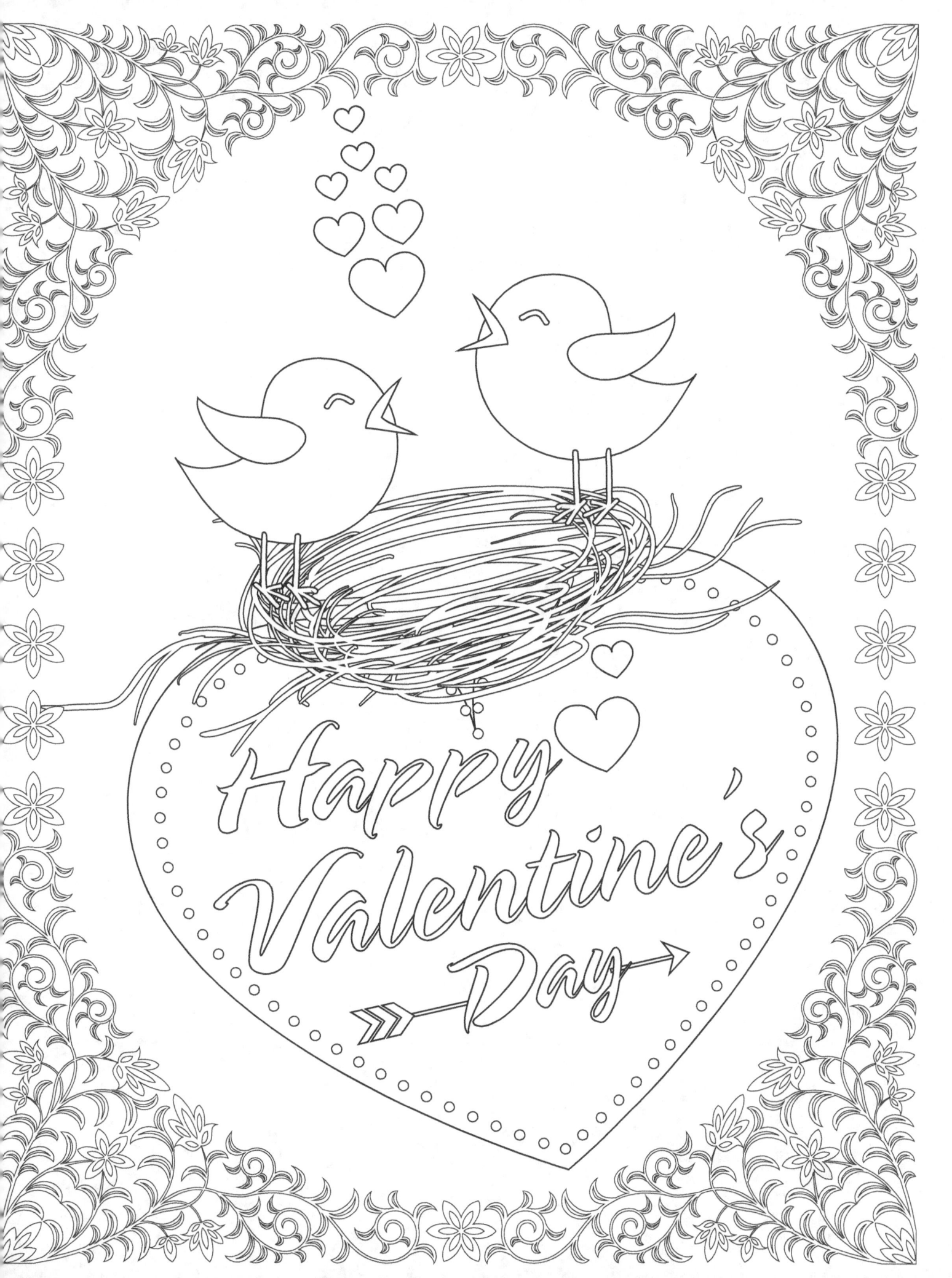

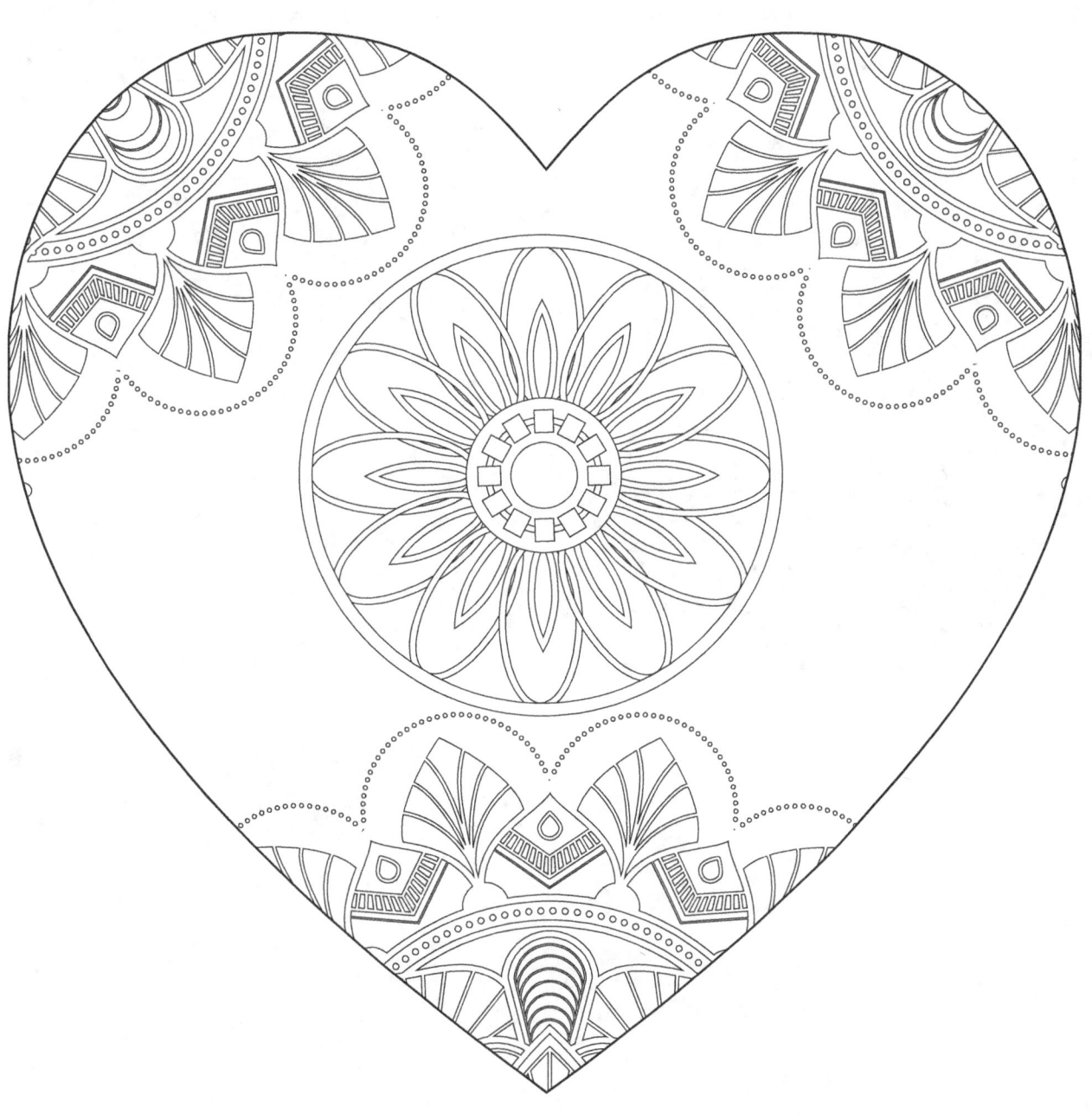

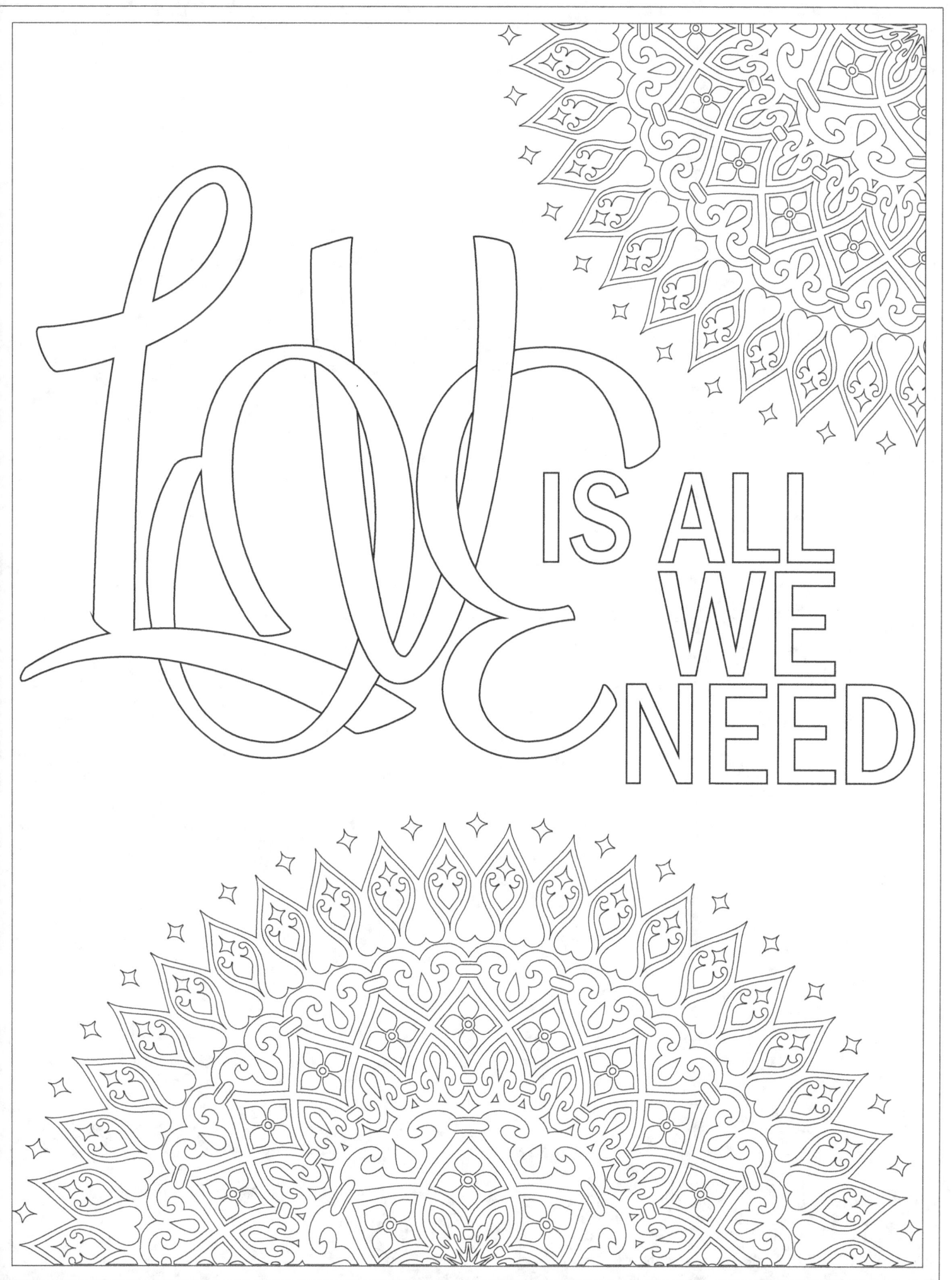

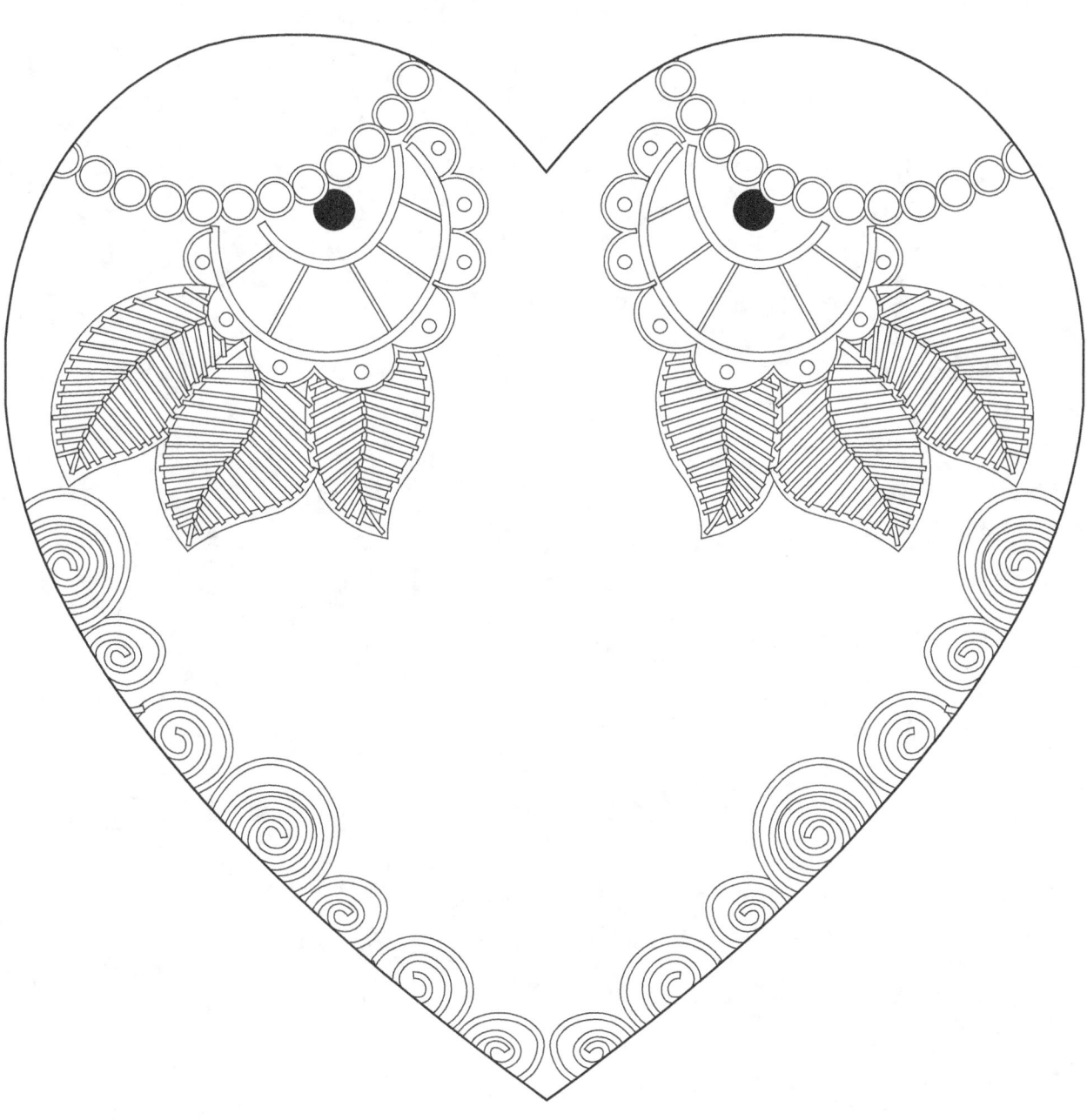

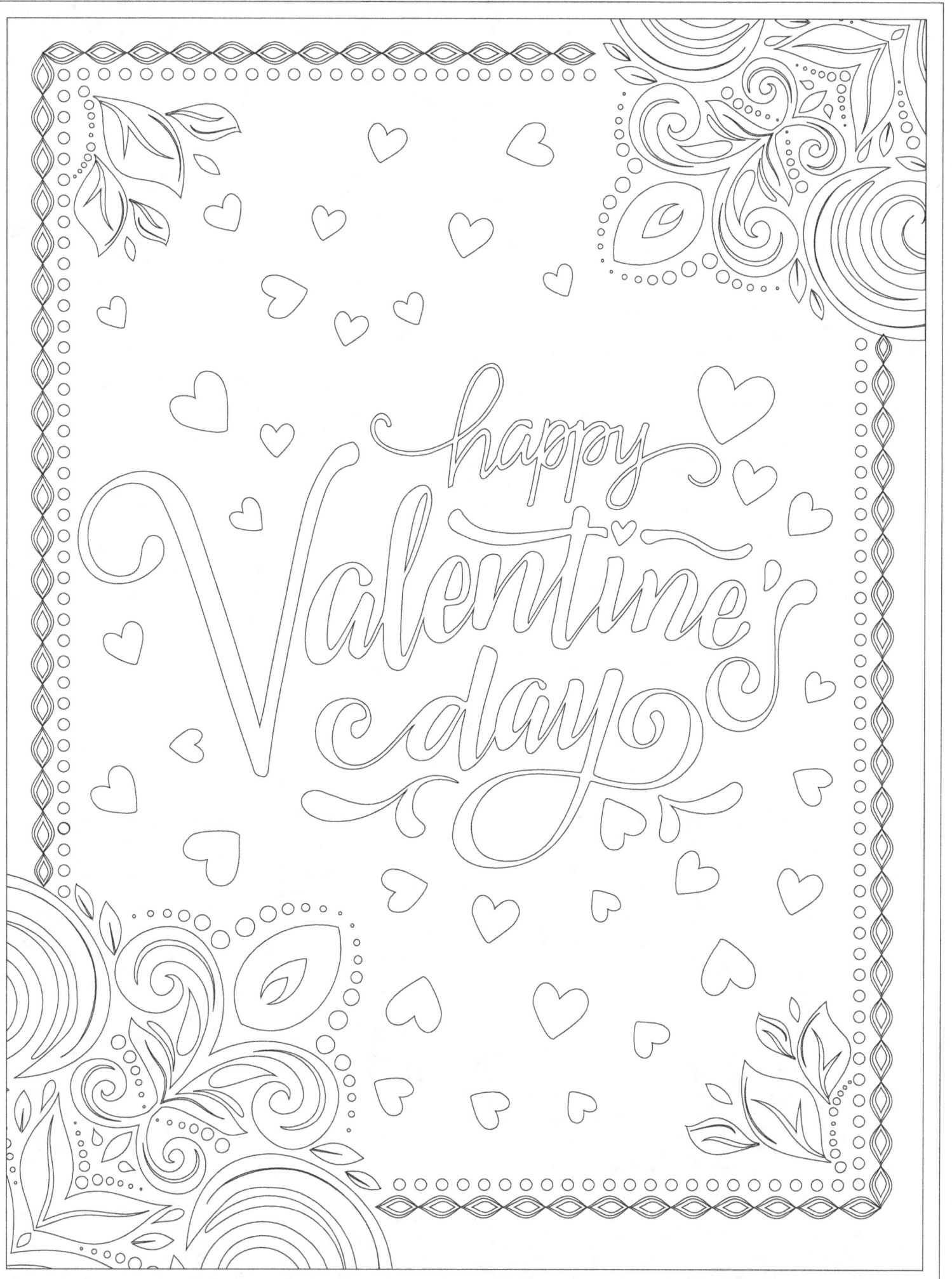

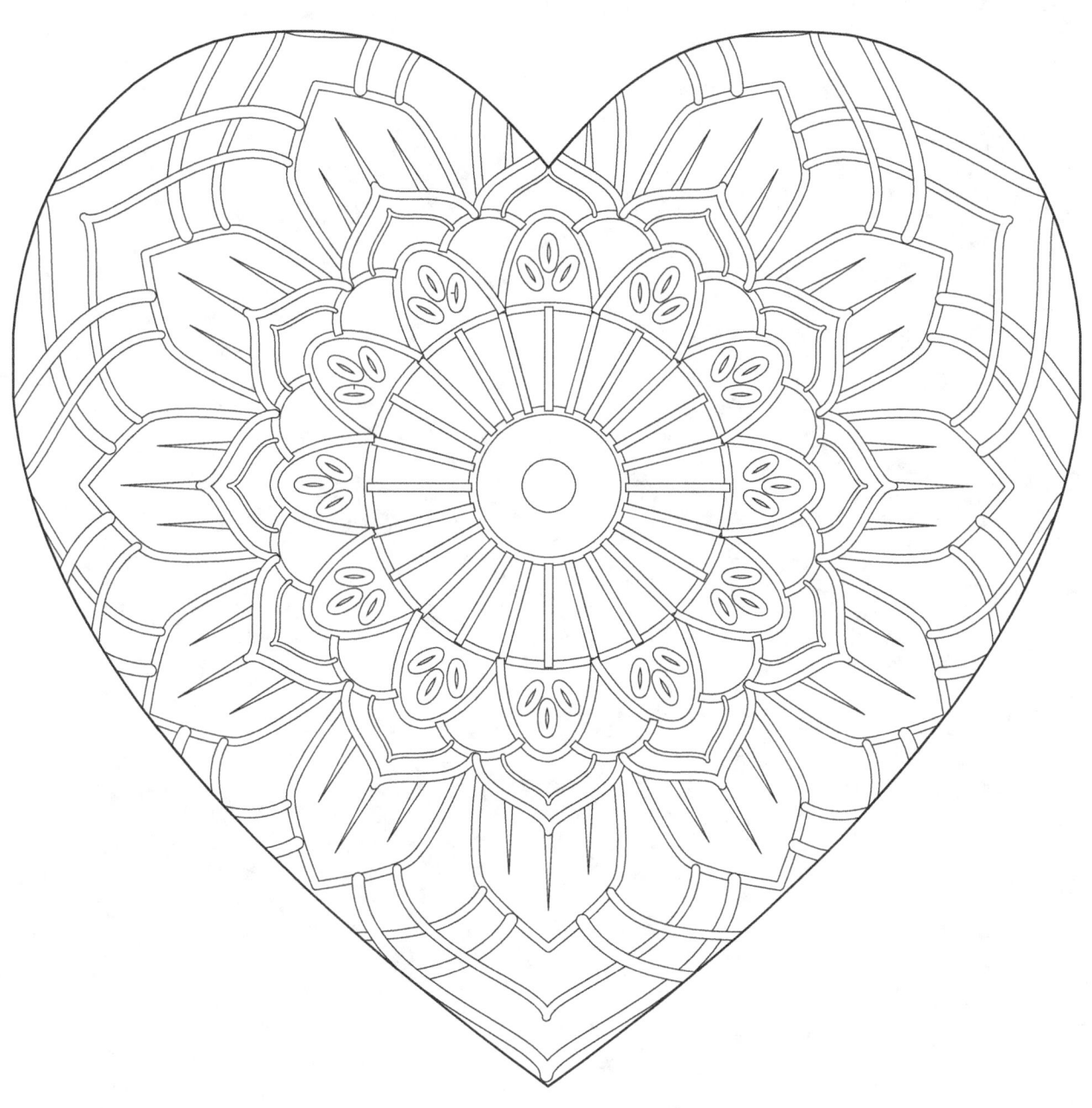

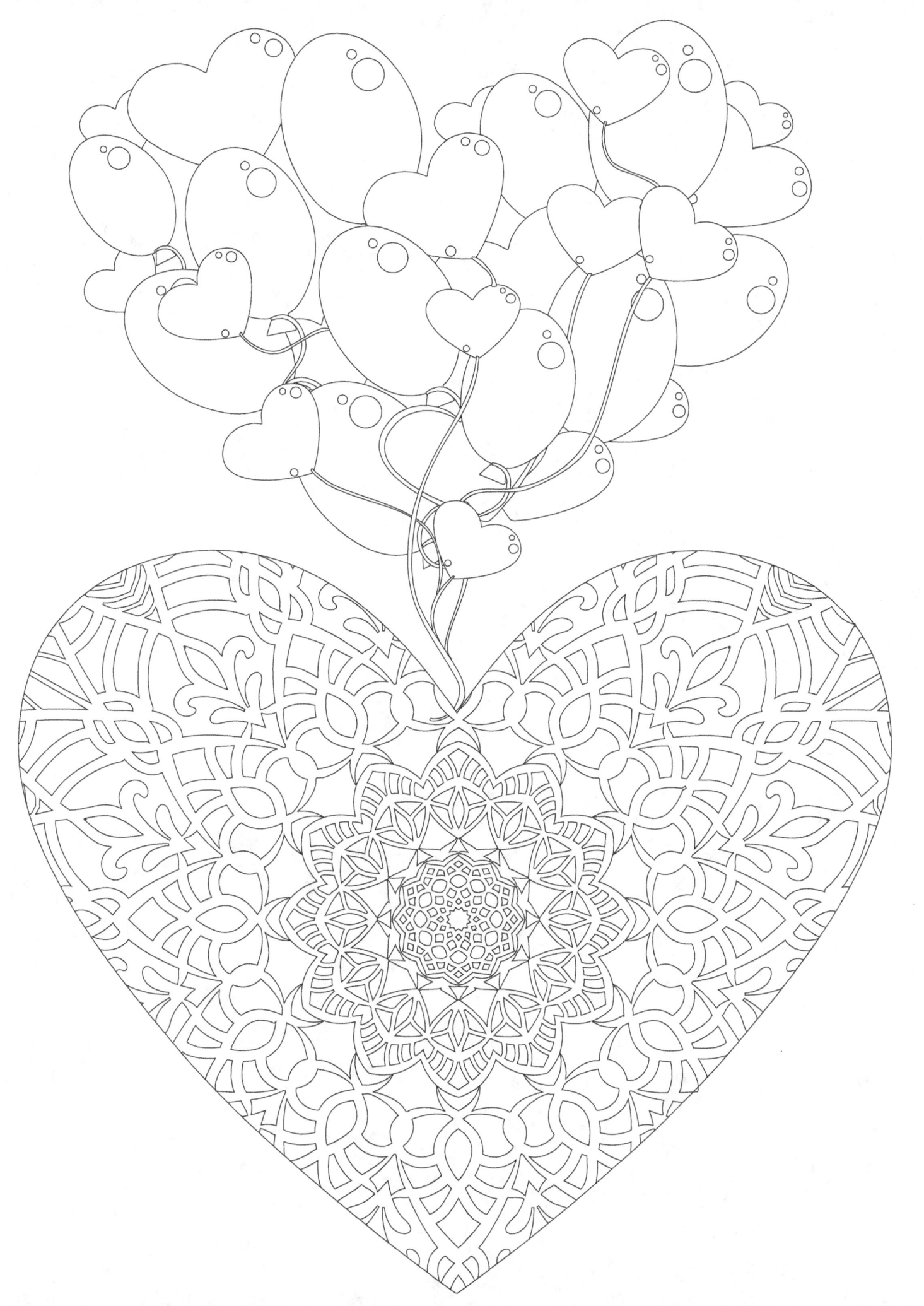

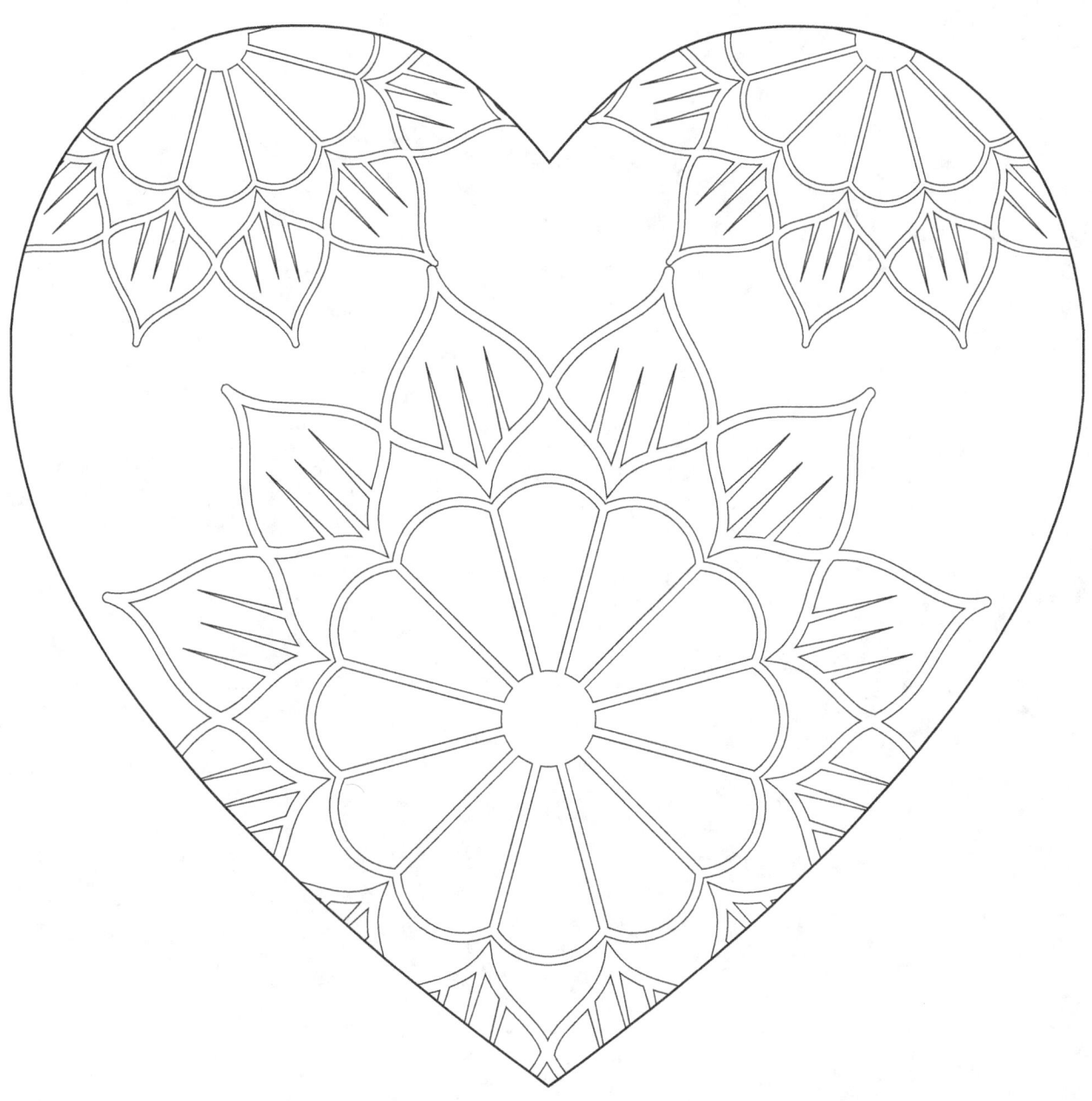

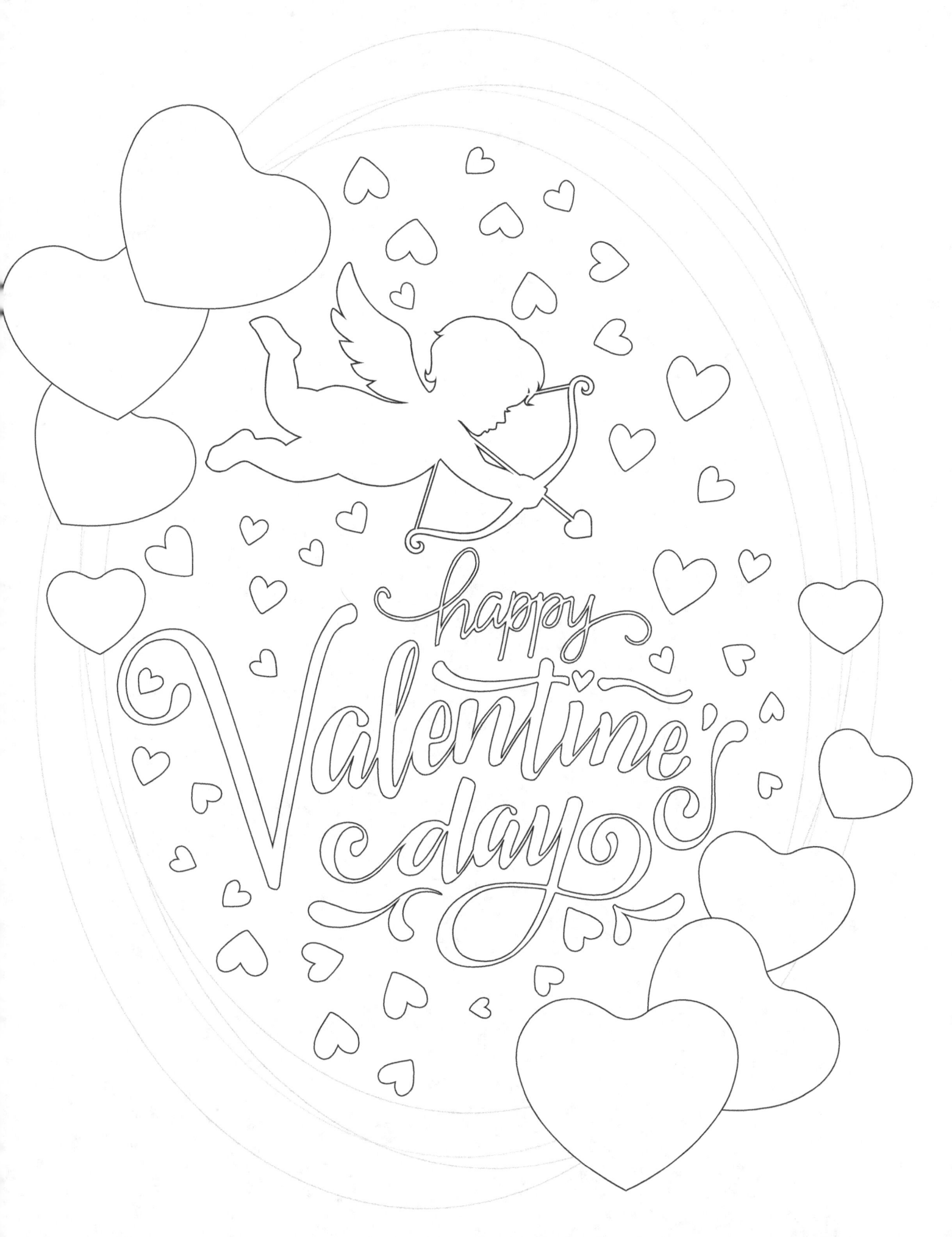

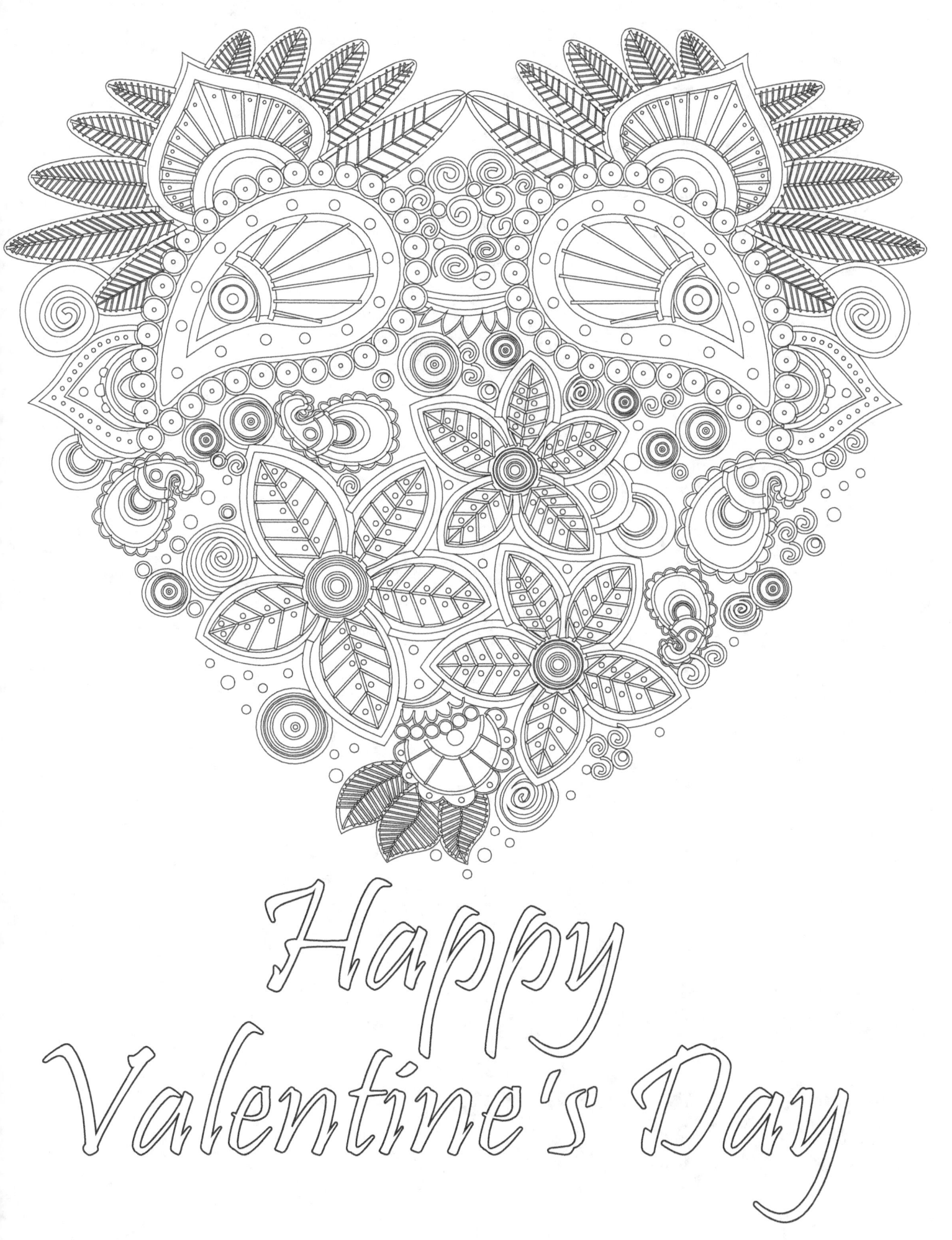

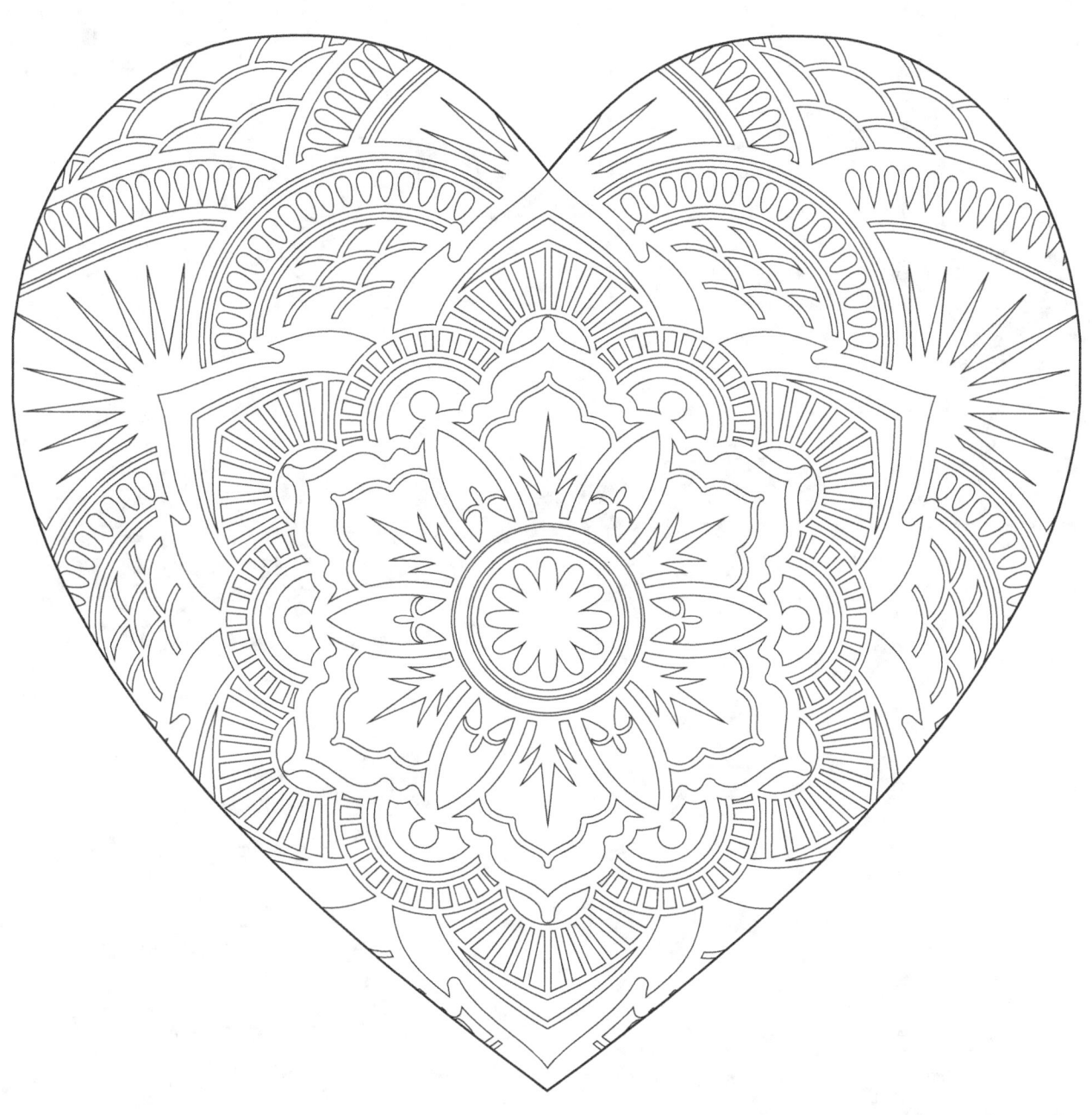

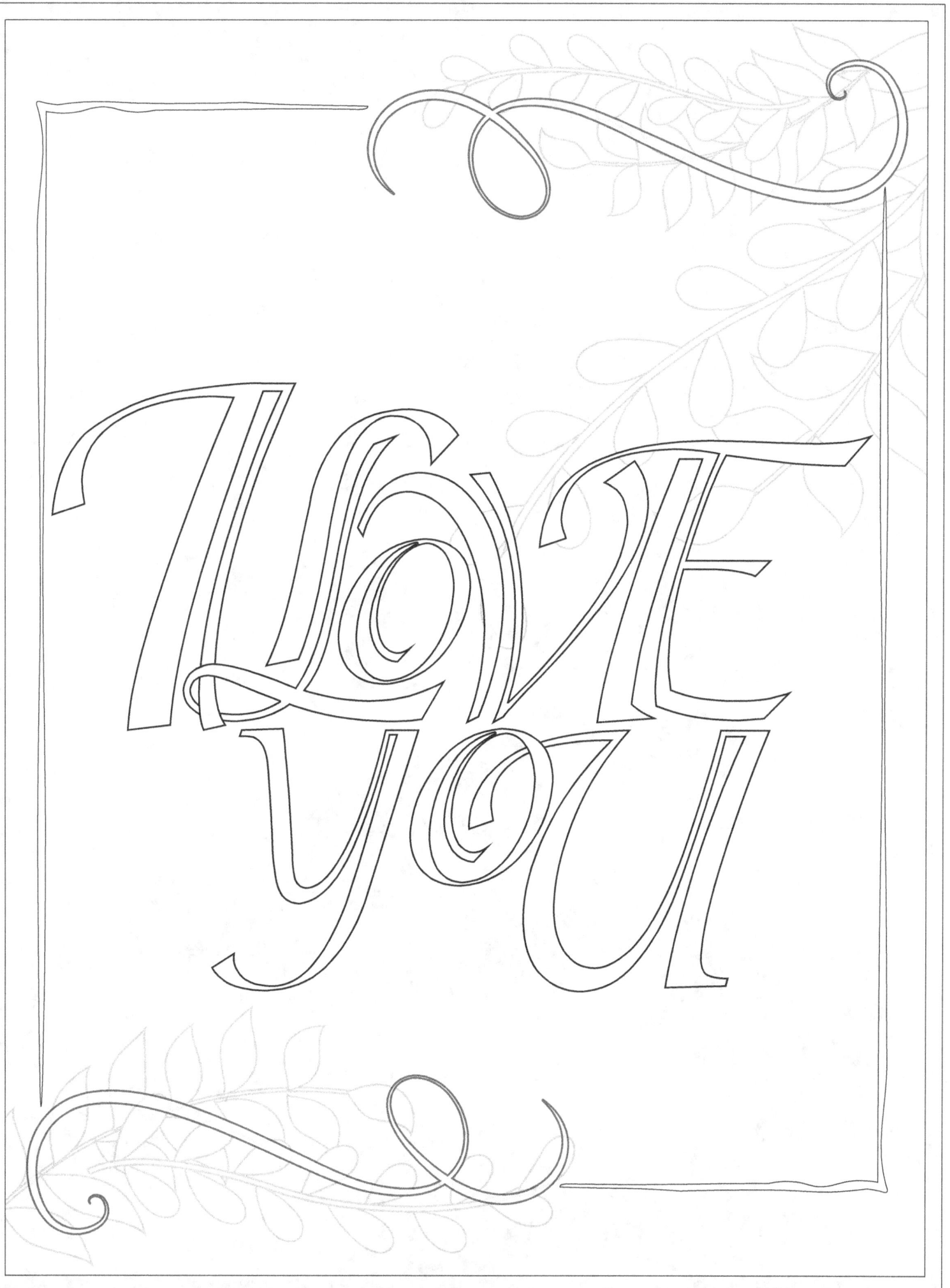

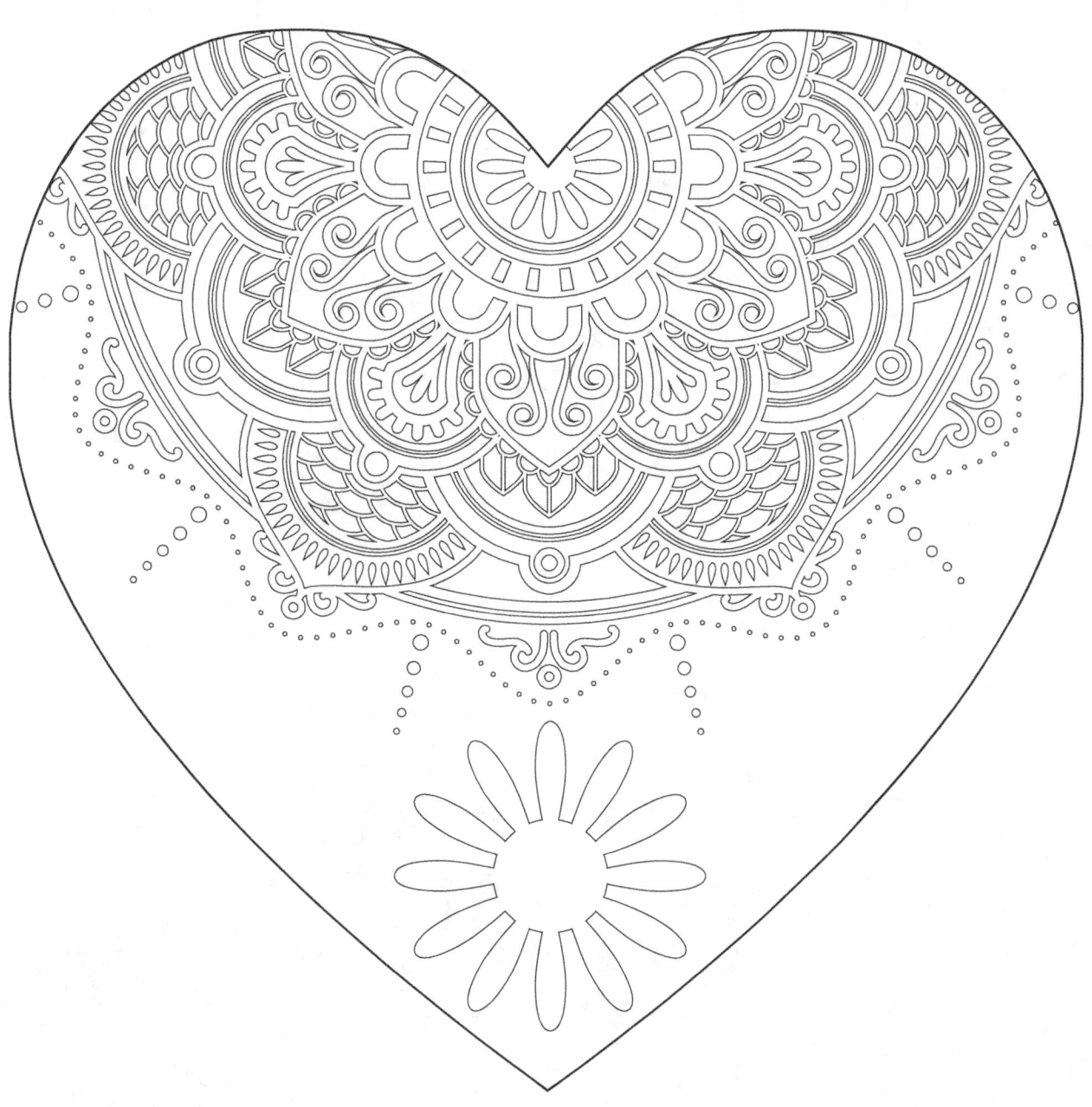

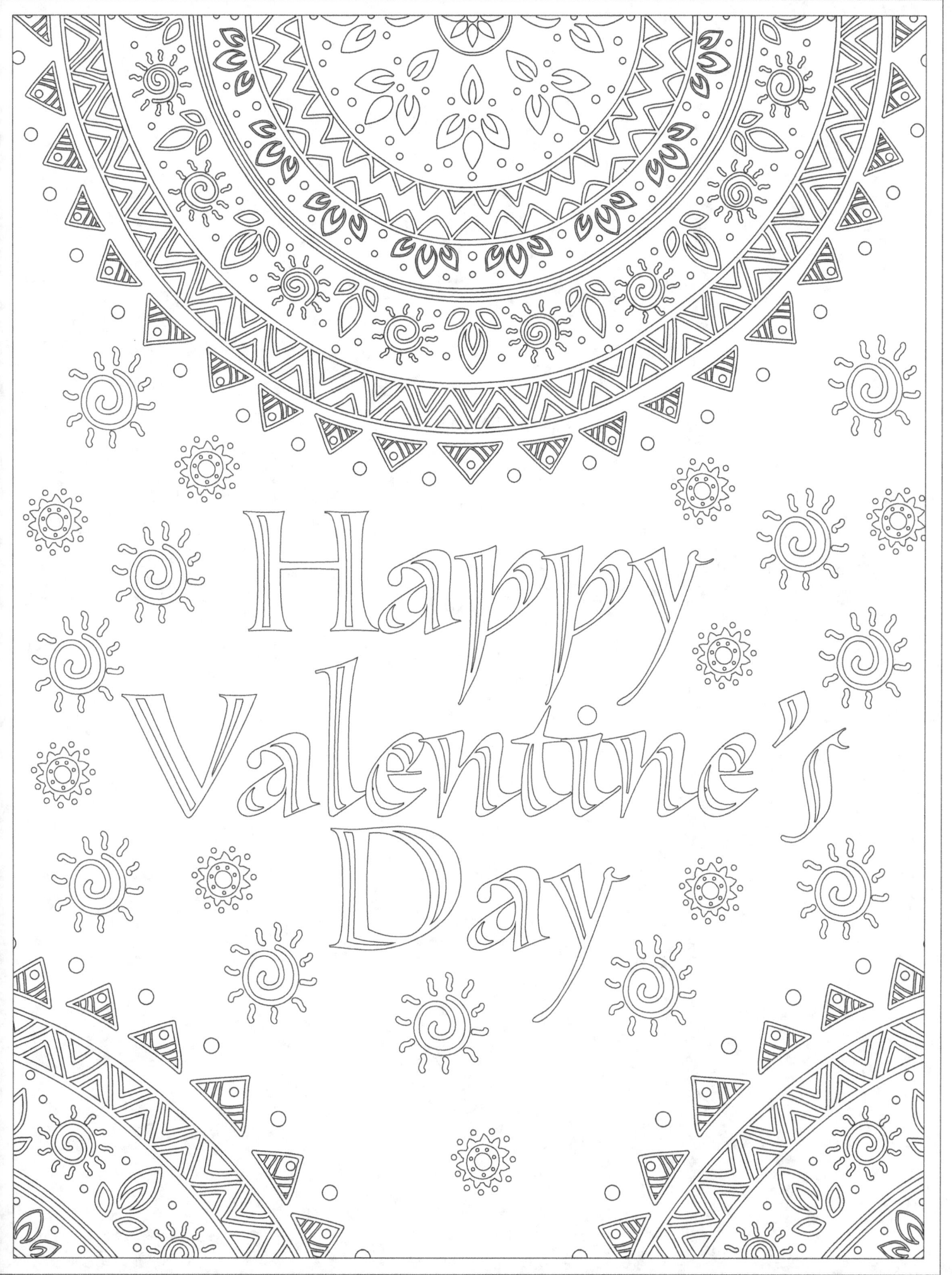

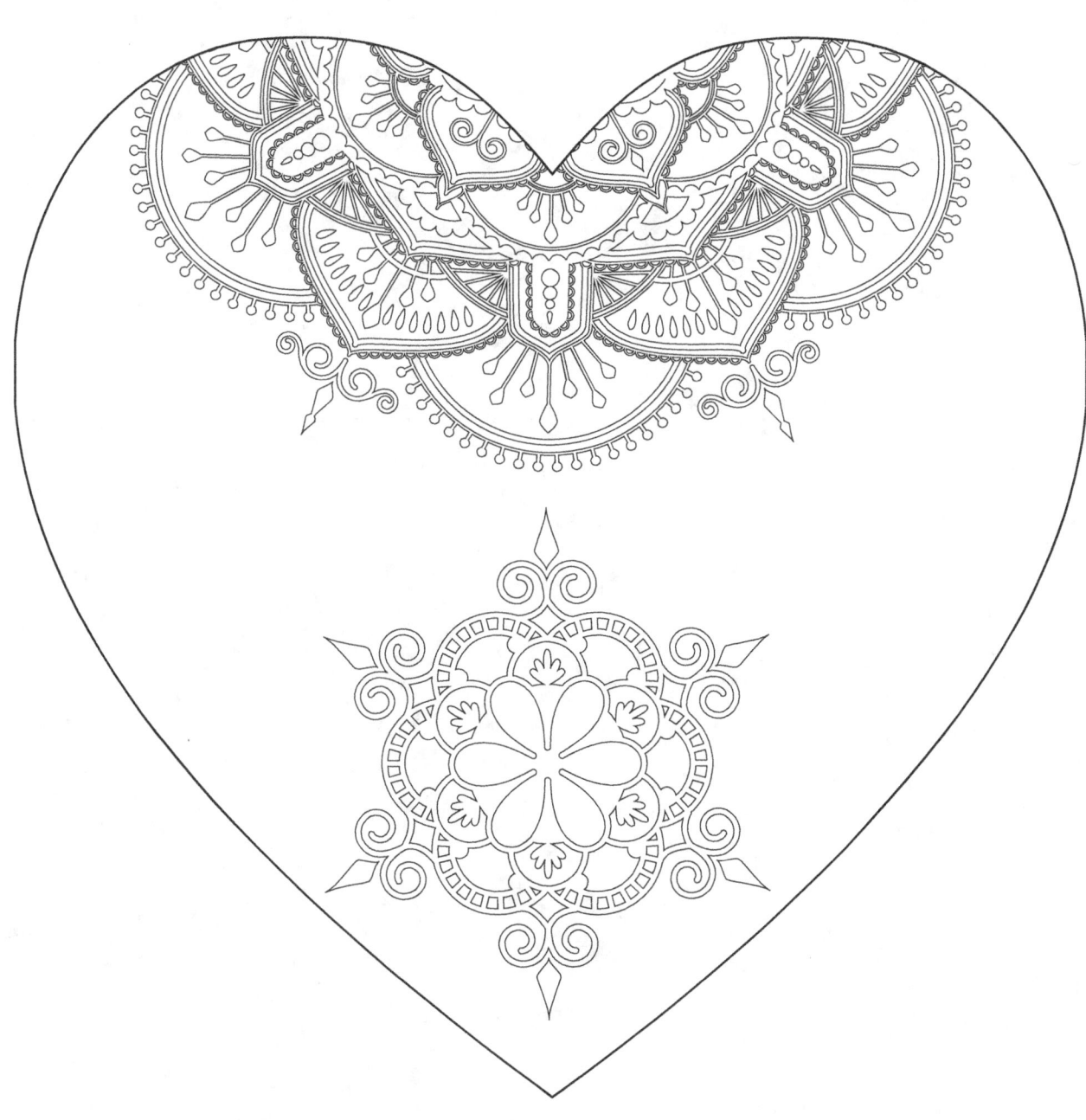

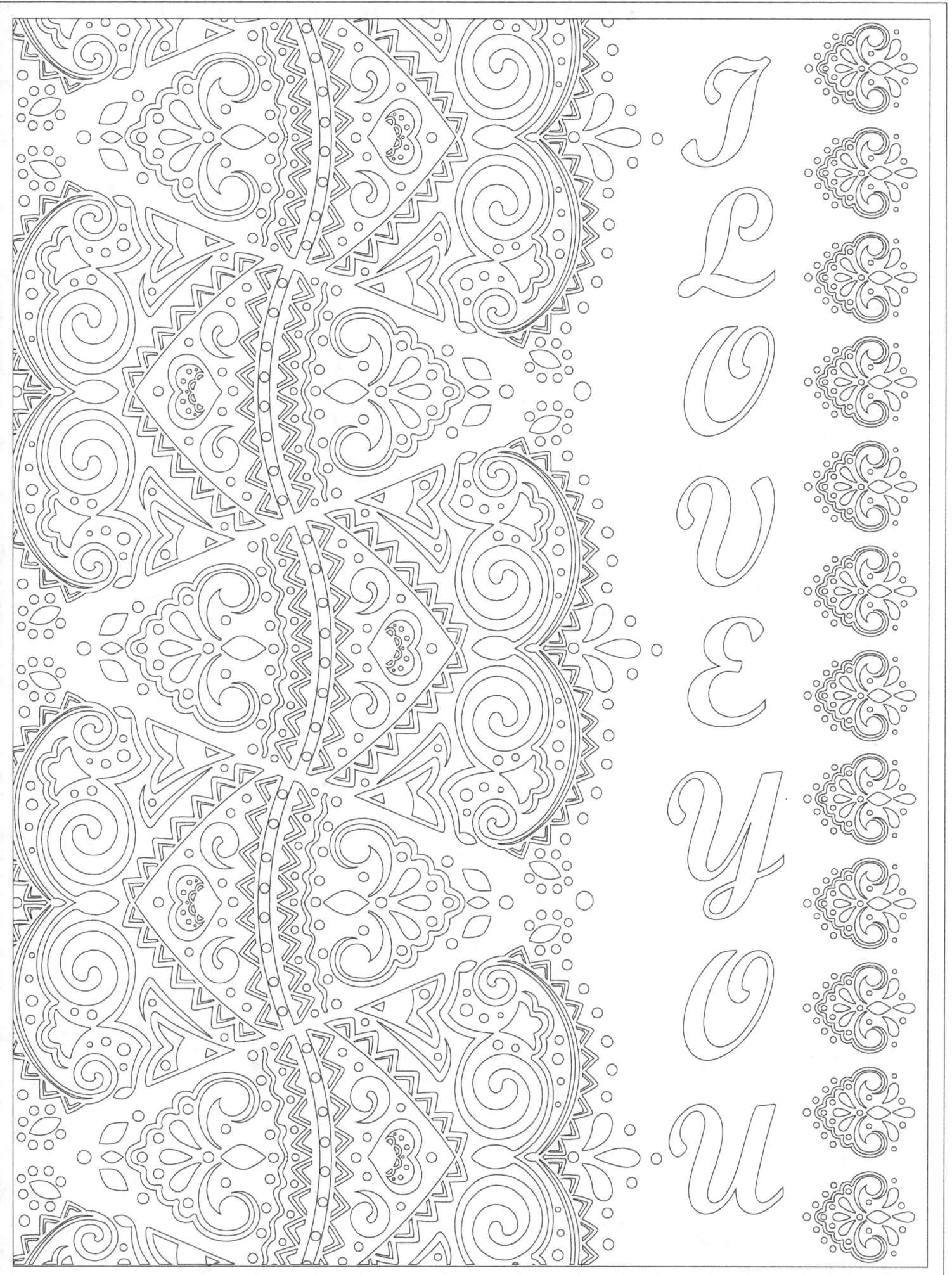

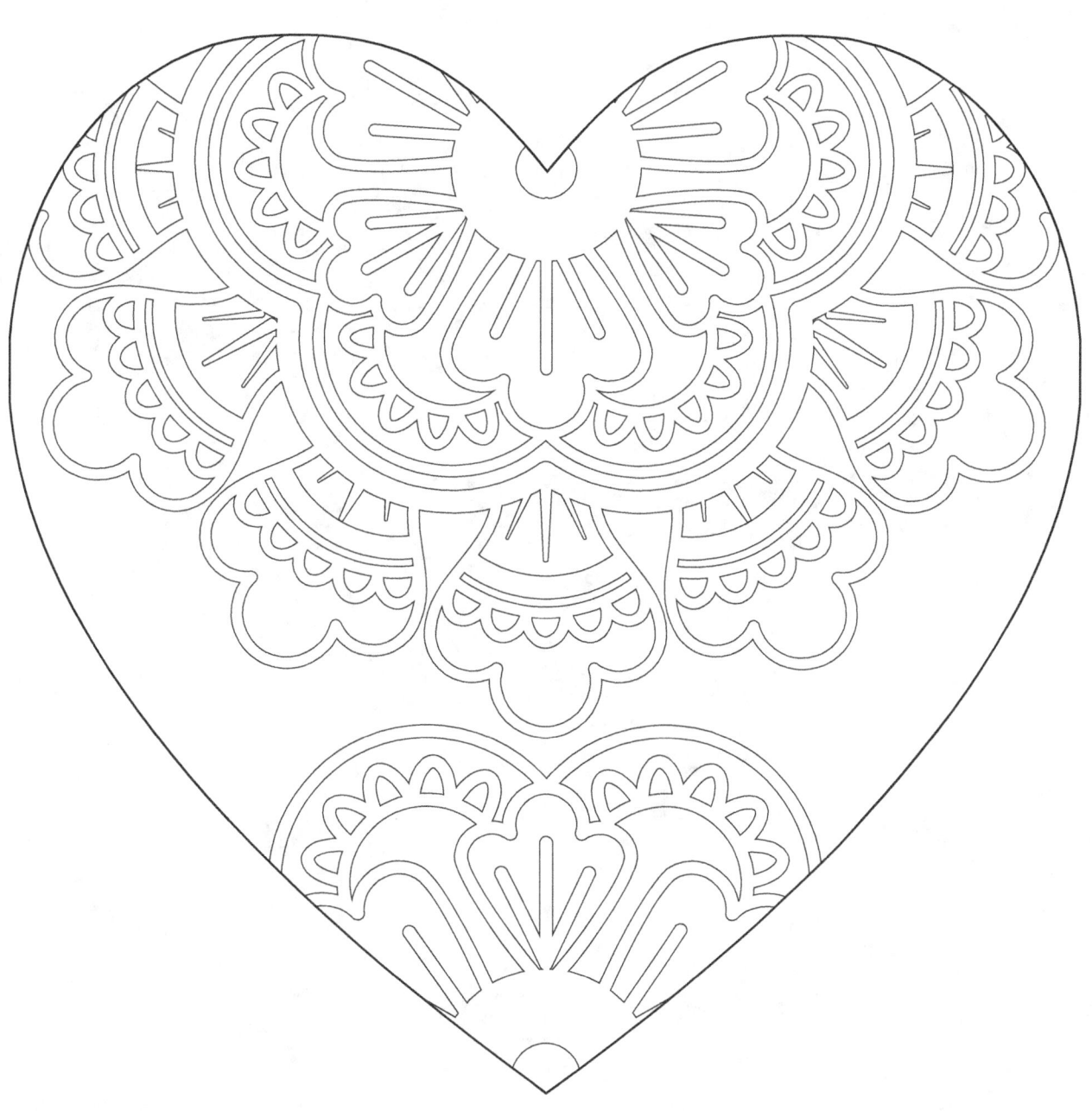

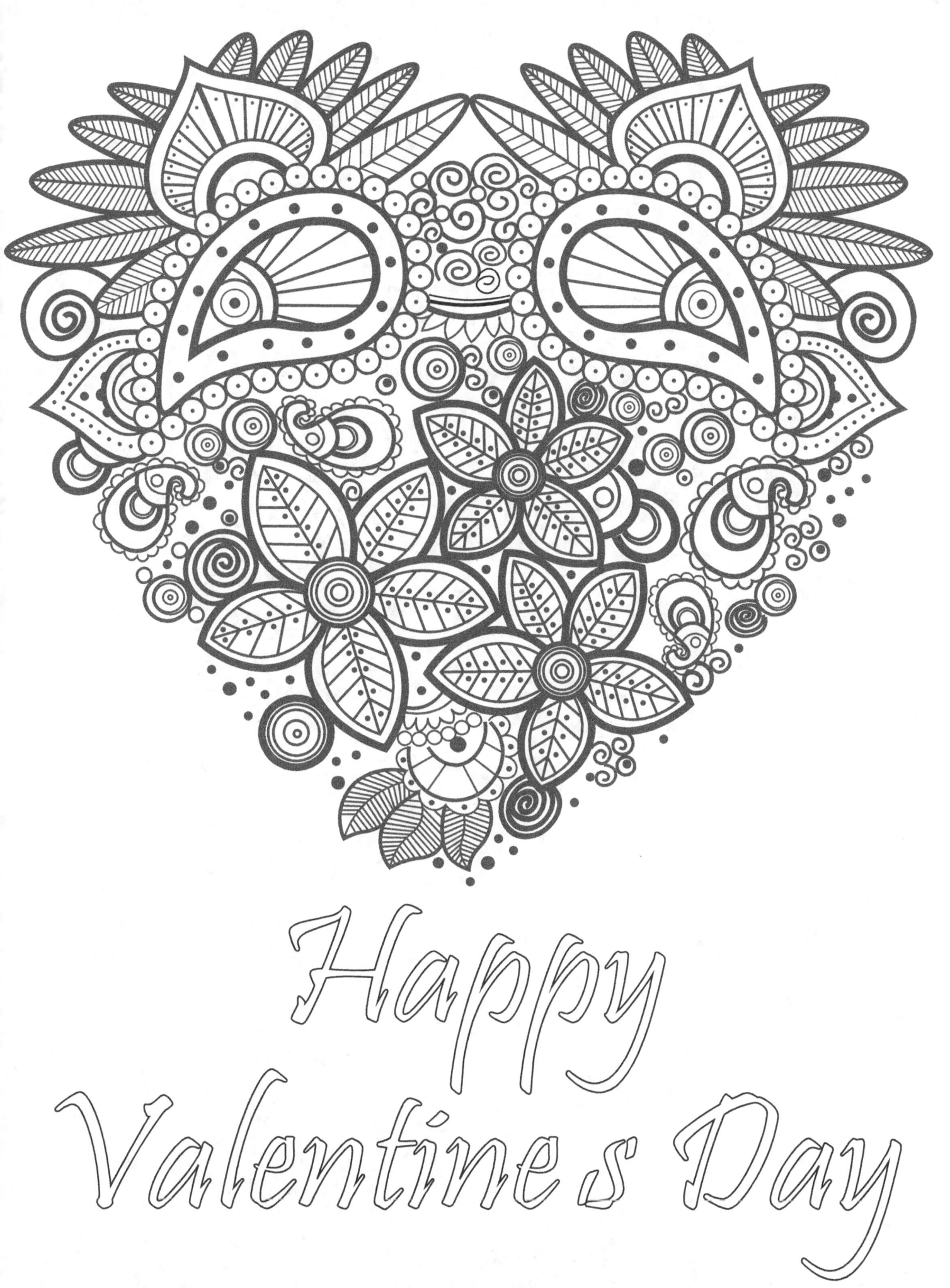

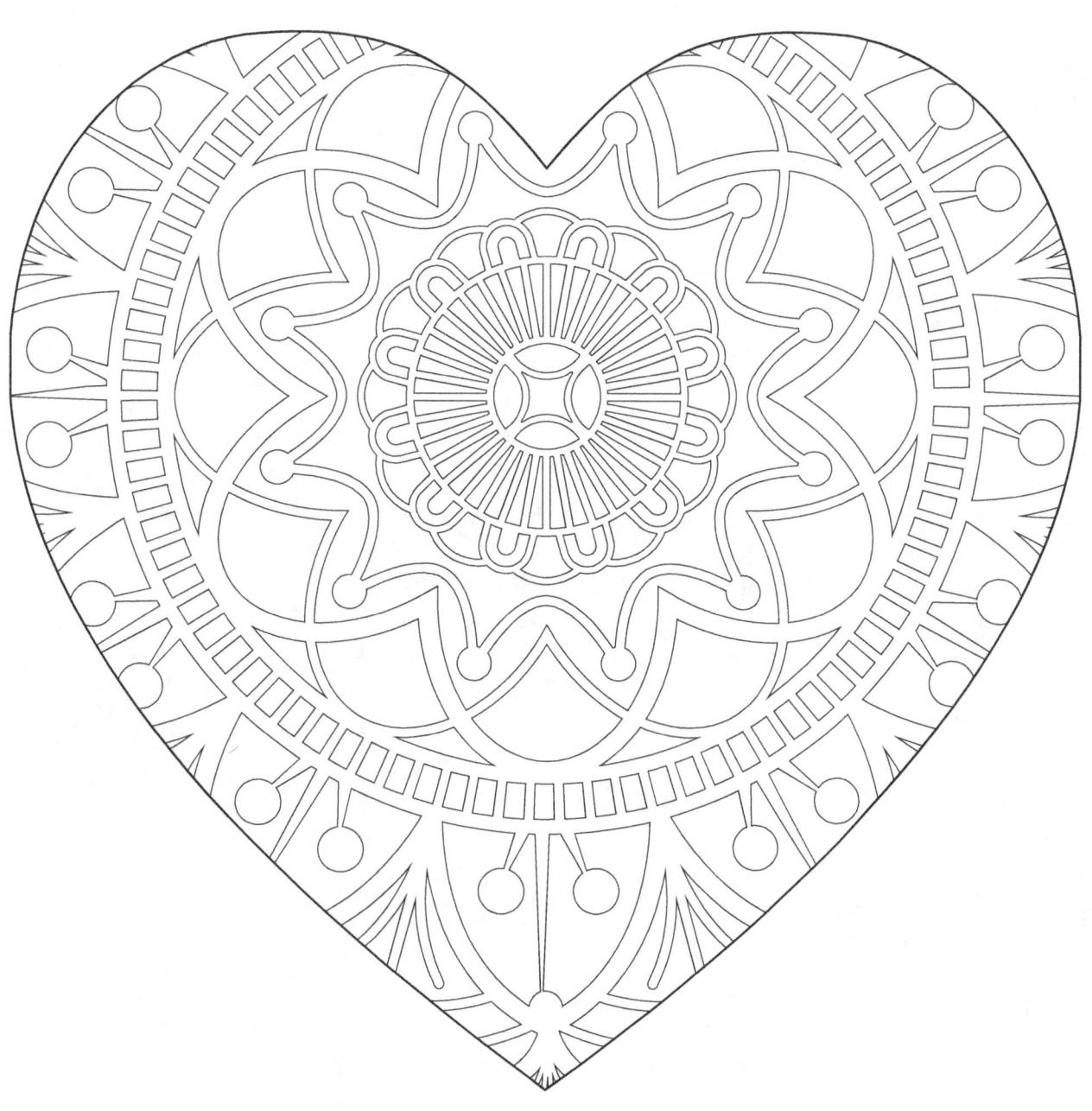

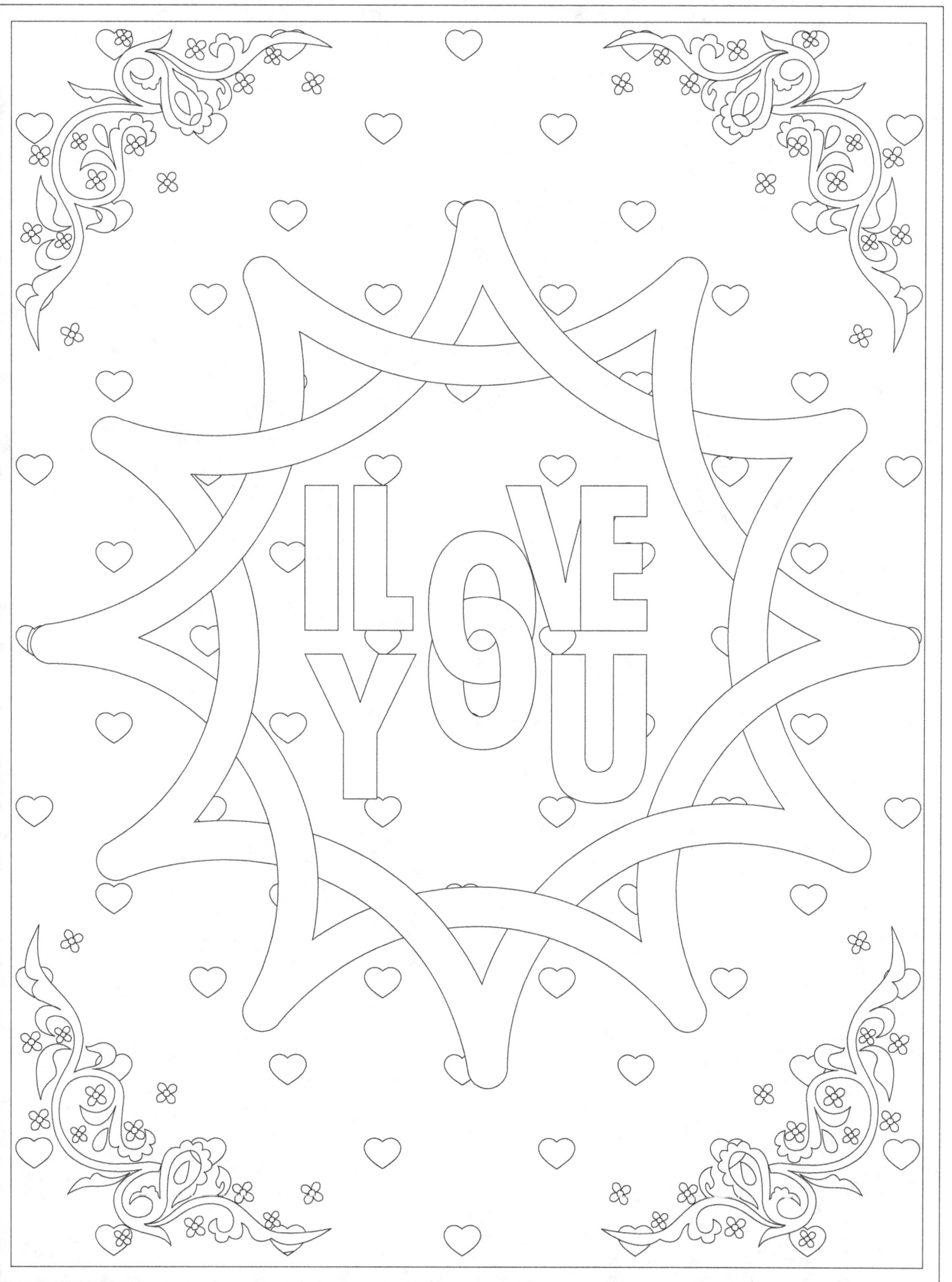

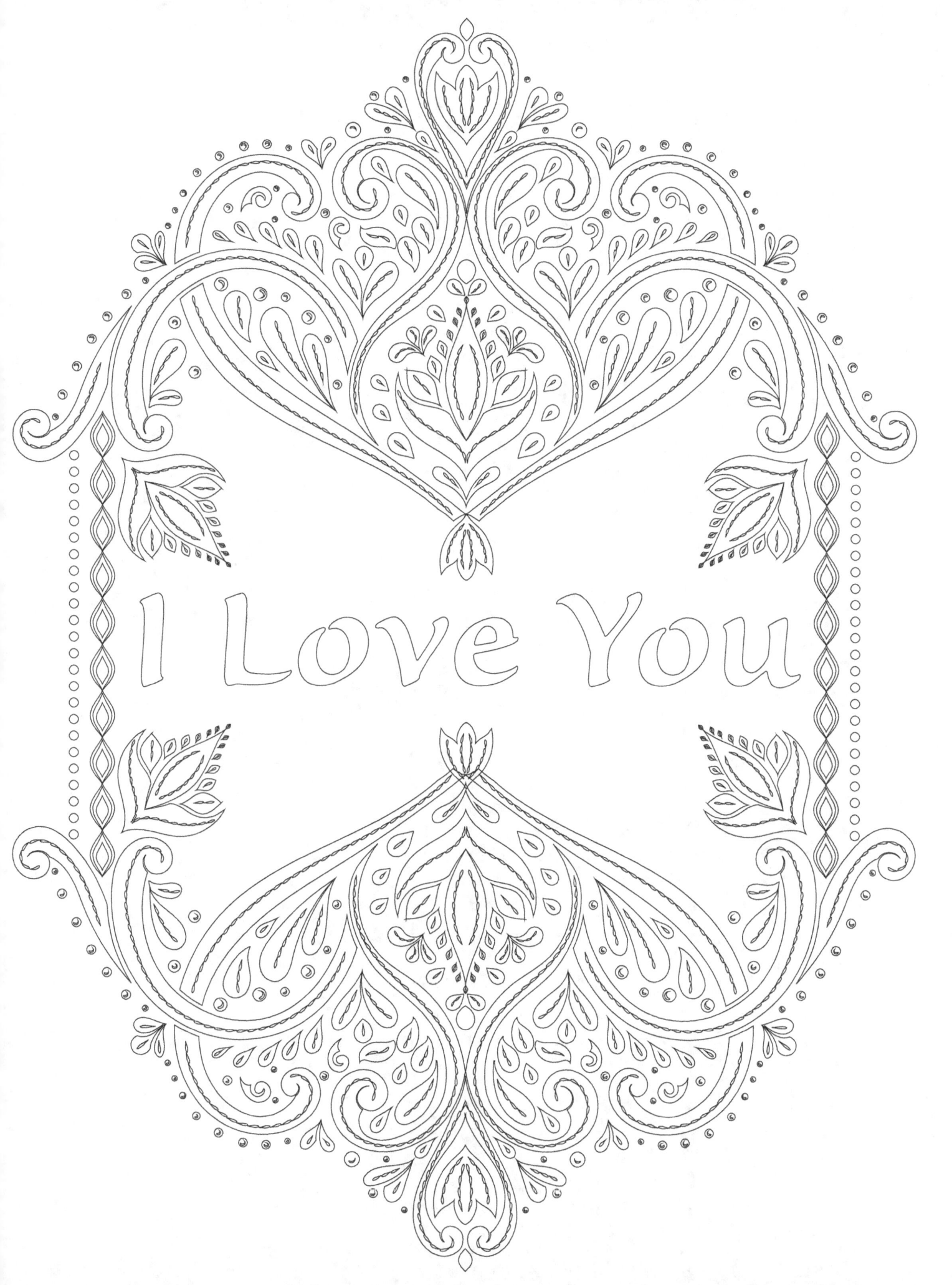

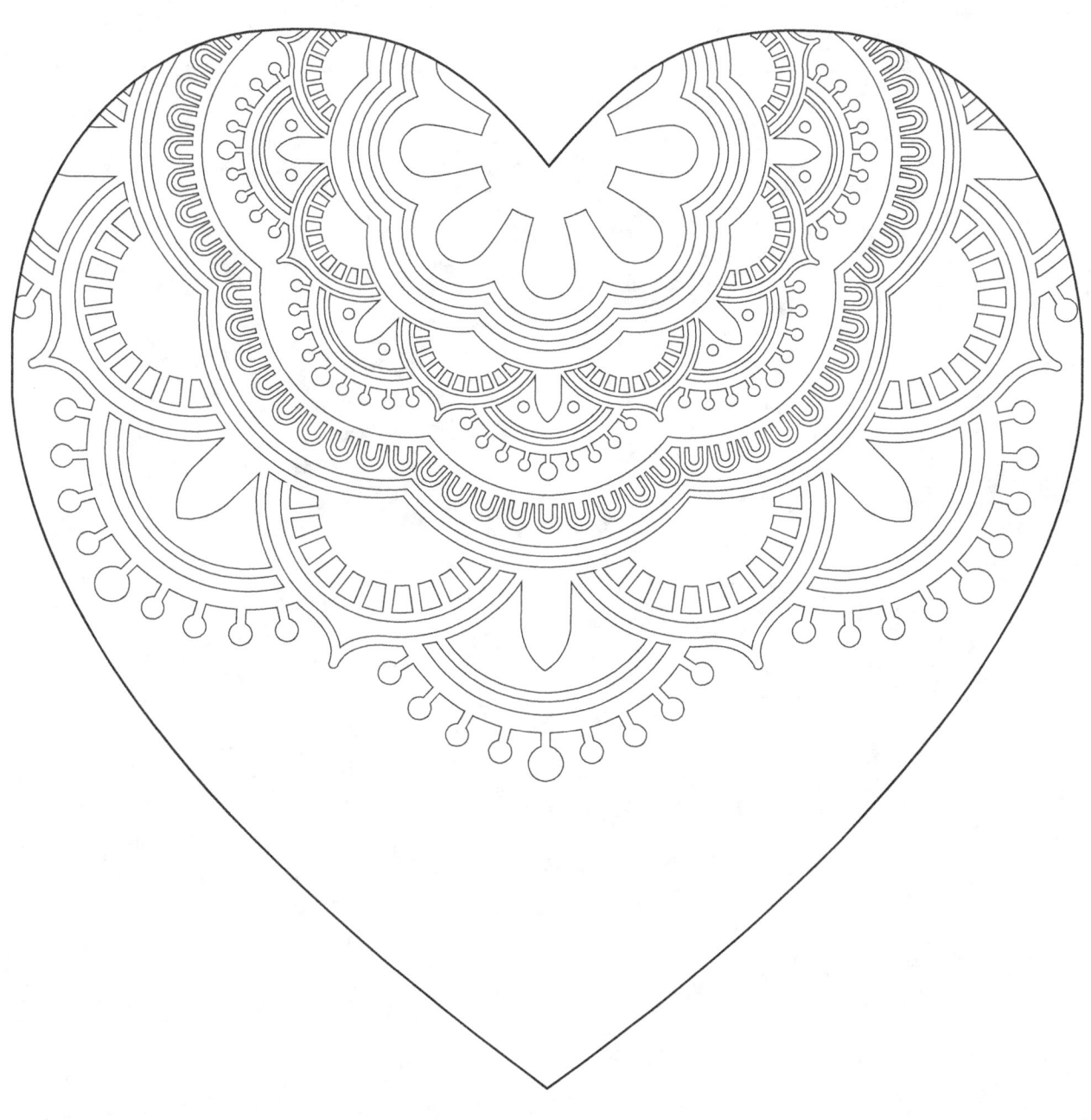

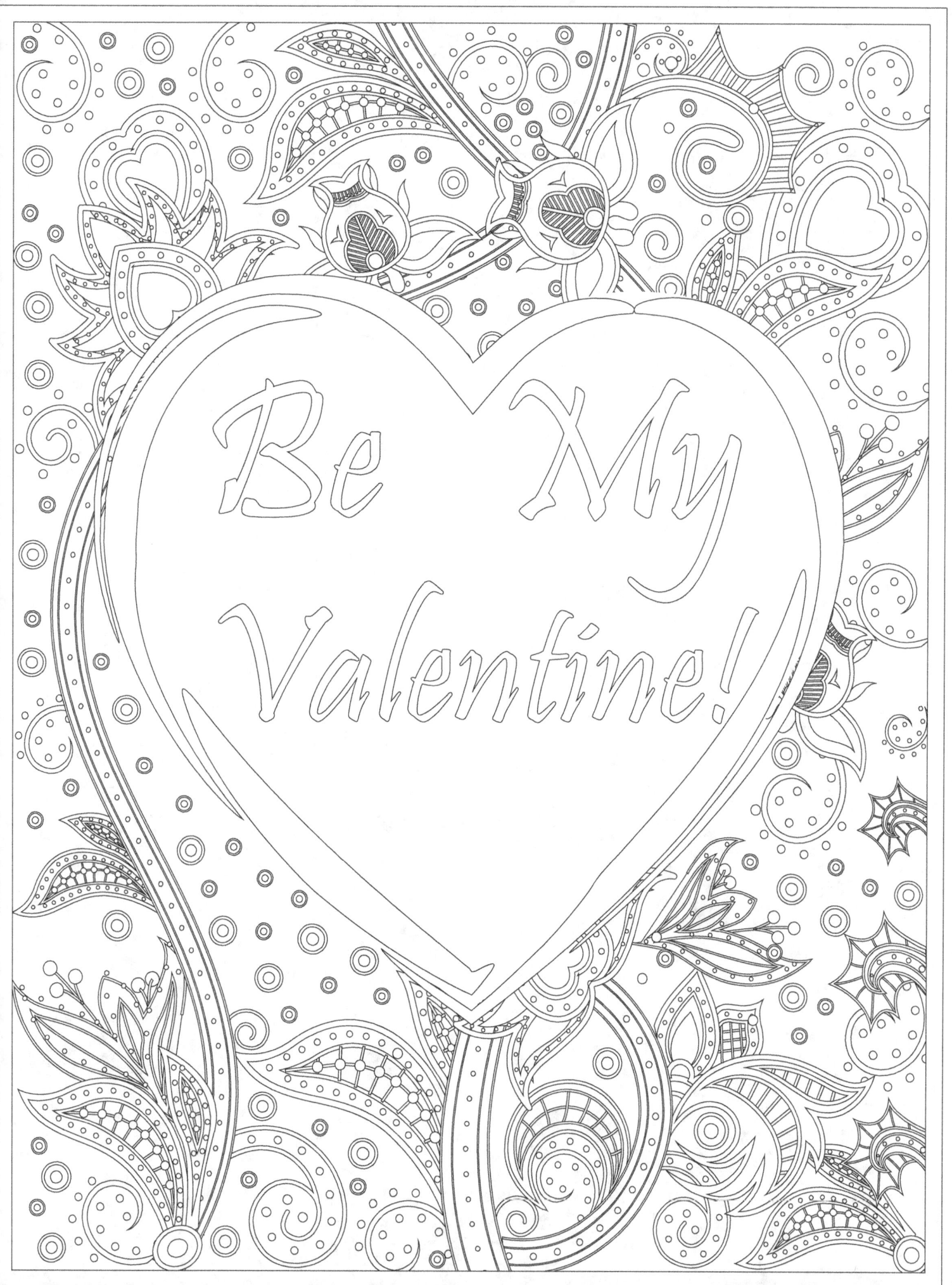

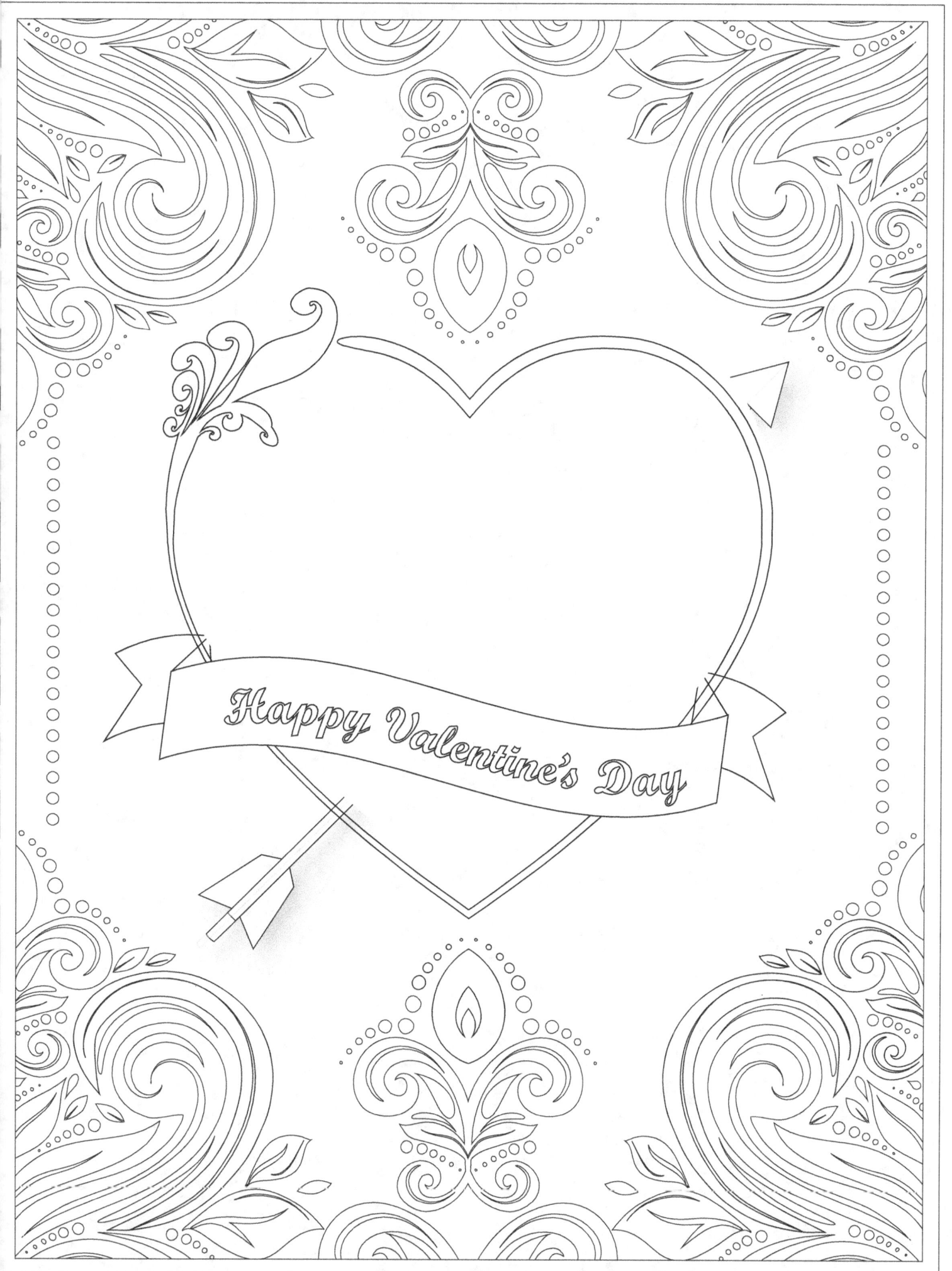

Happy Valentine's Day

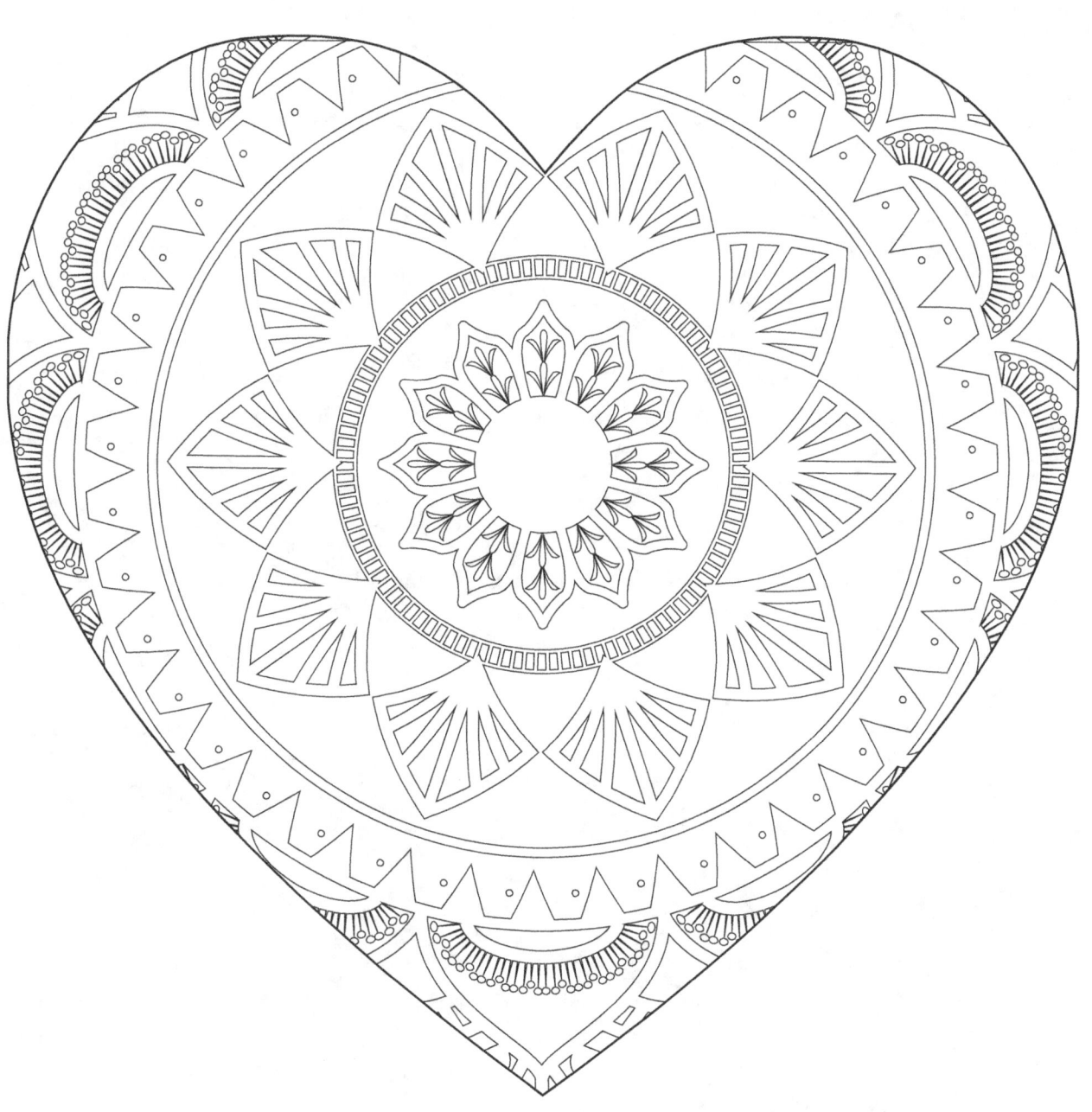

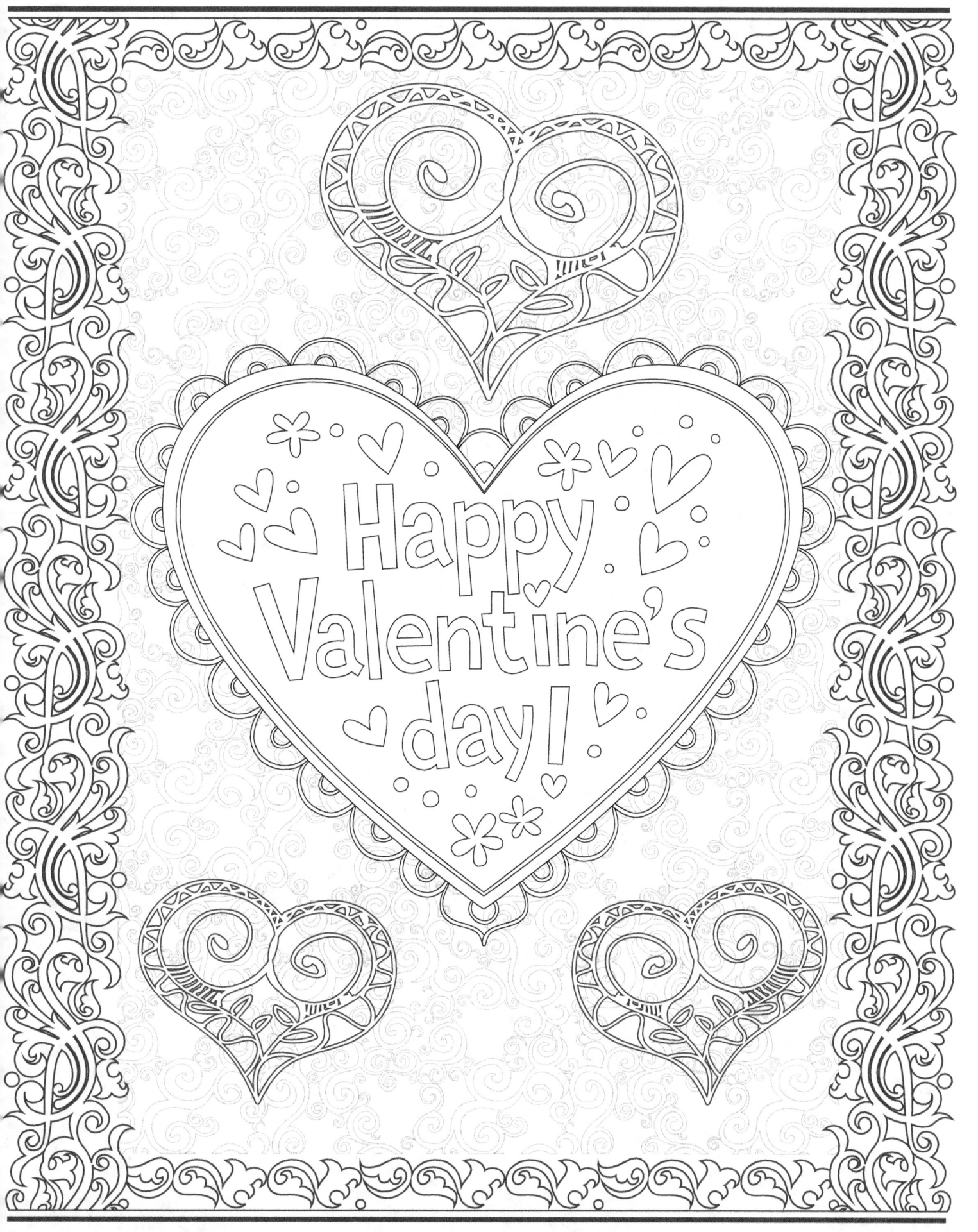

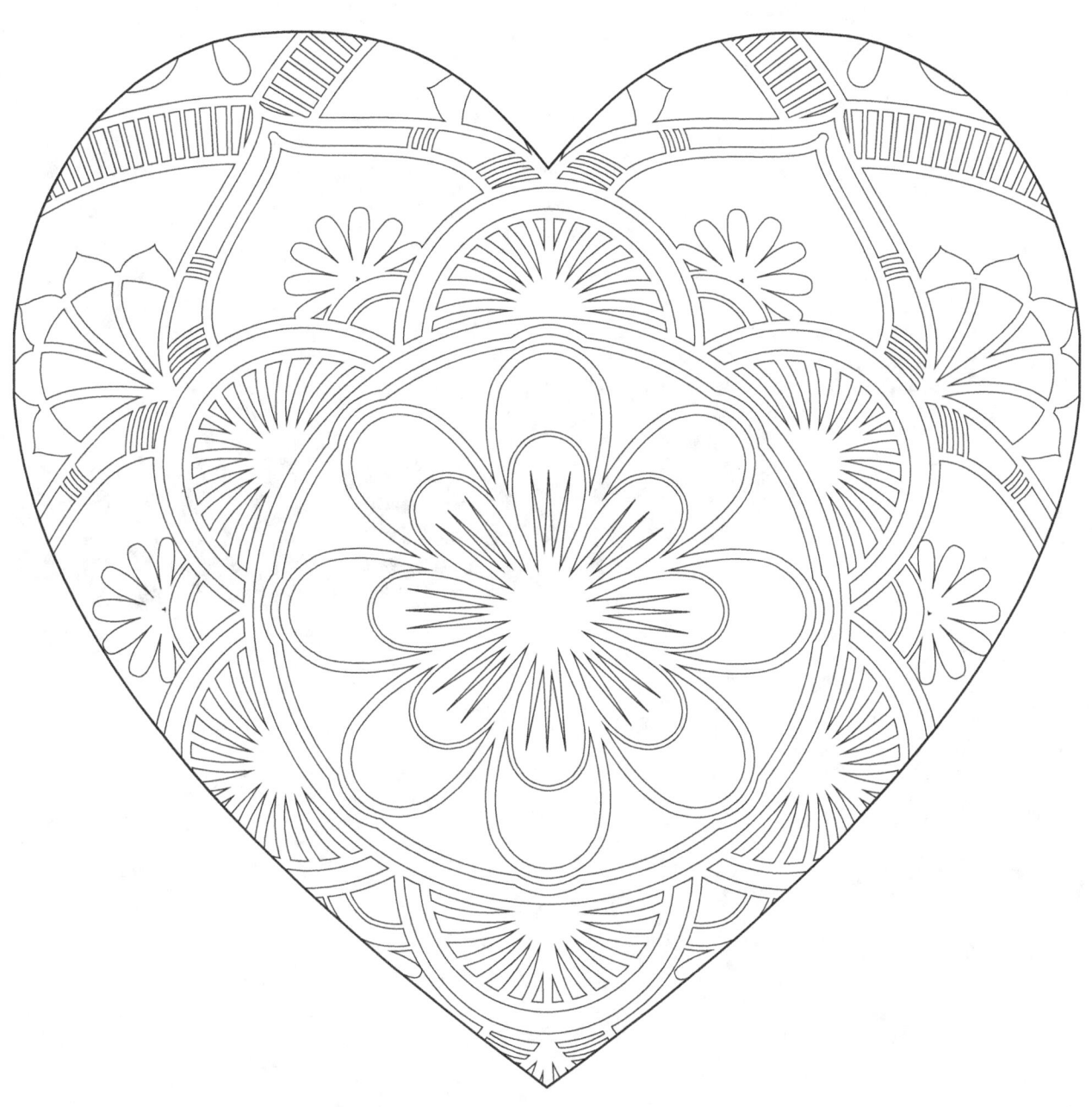

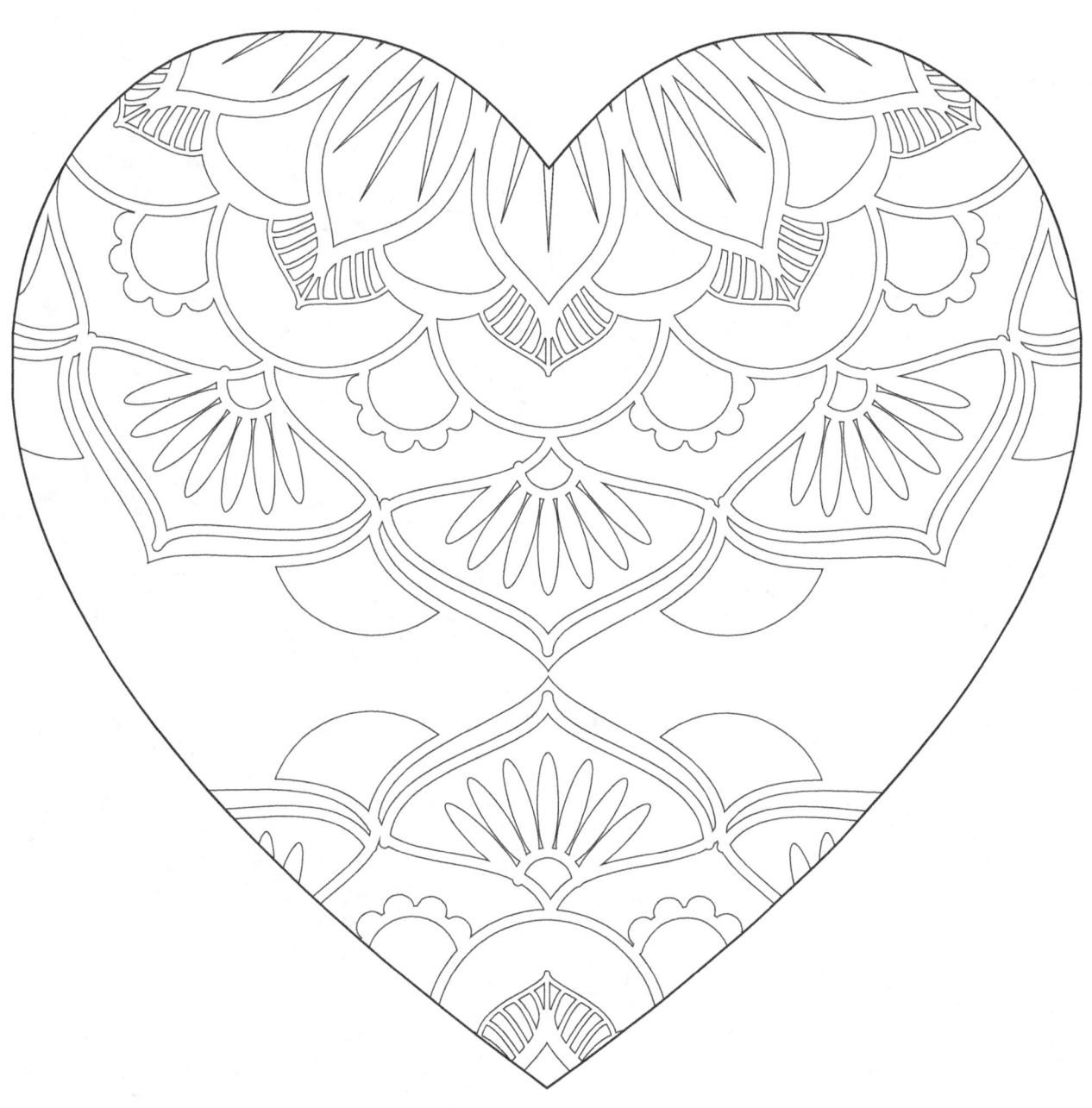

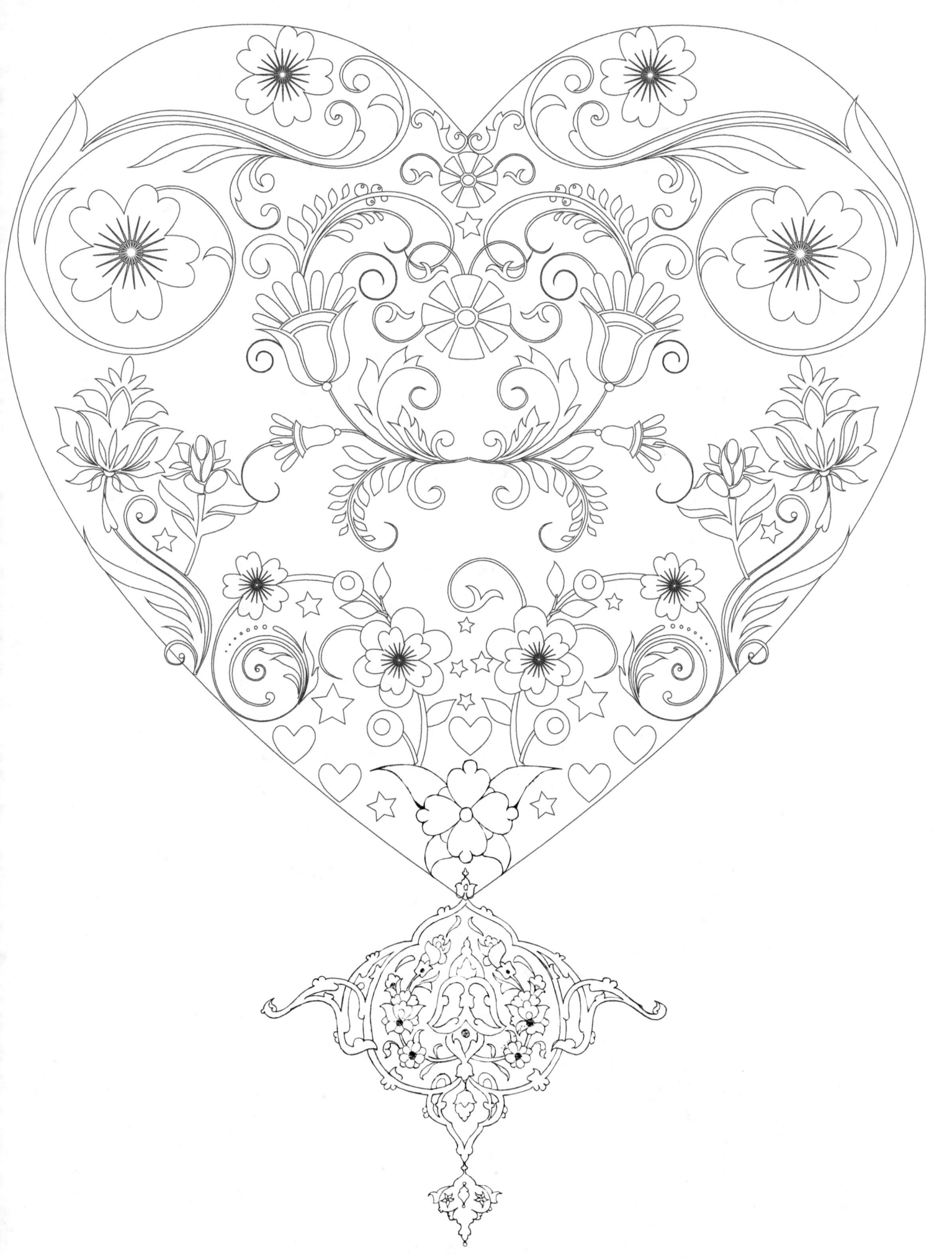

BE ♥ MY VALENTINE

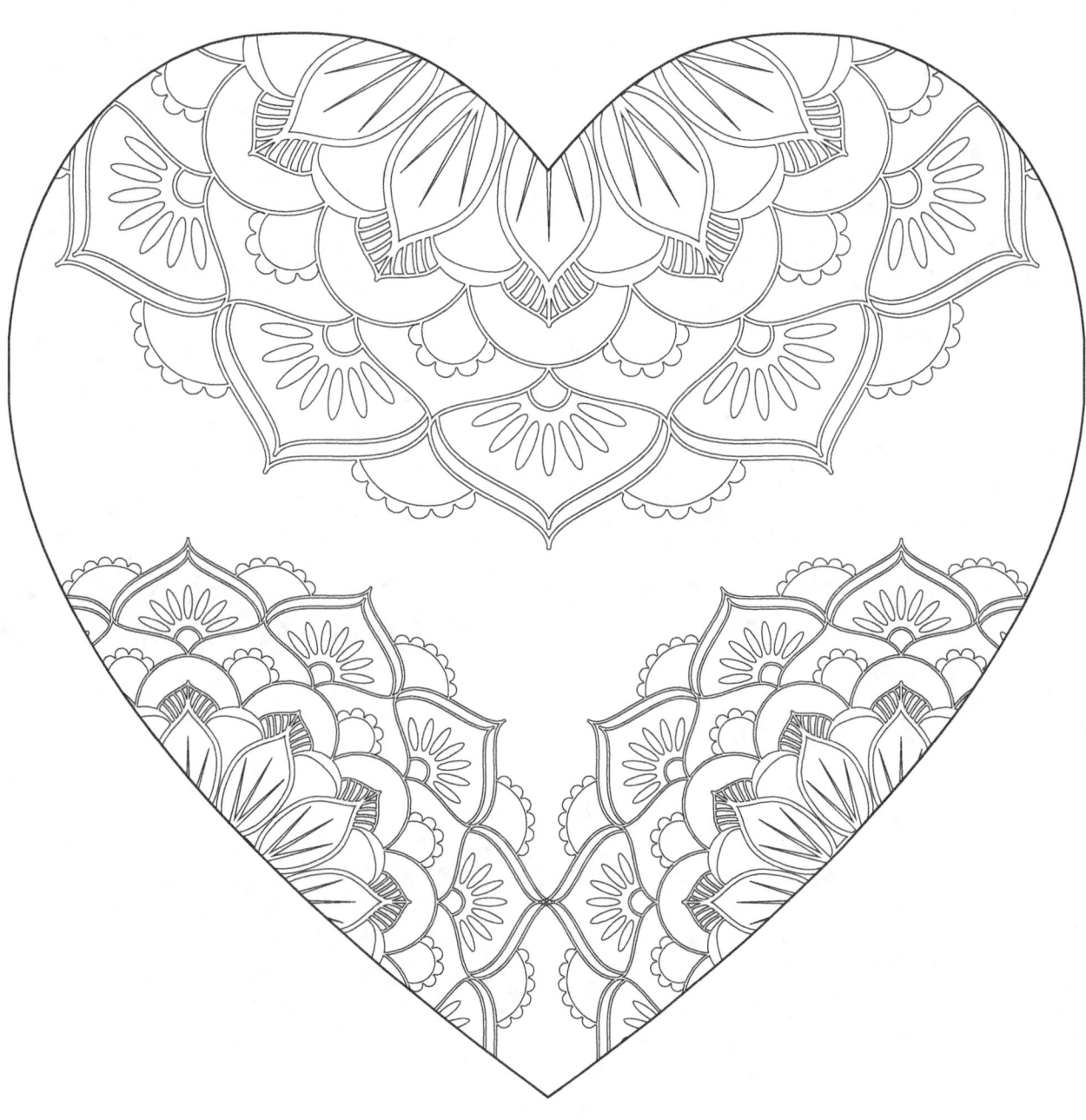

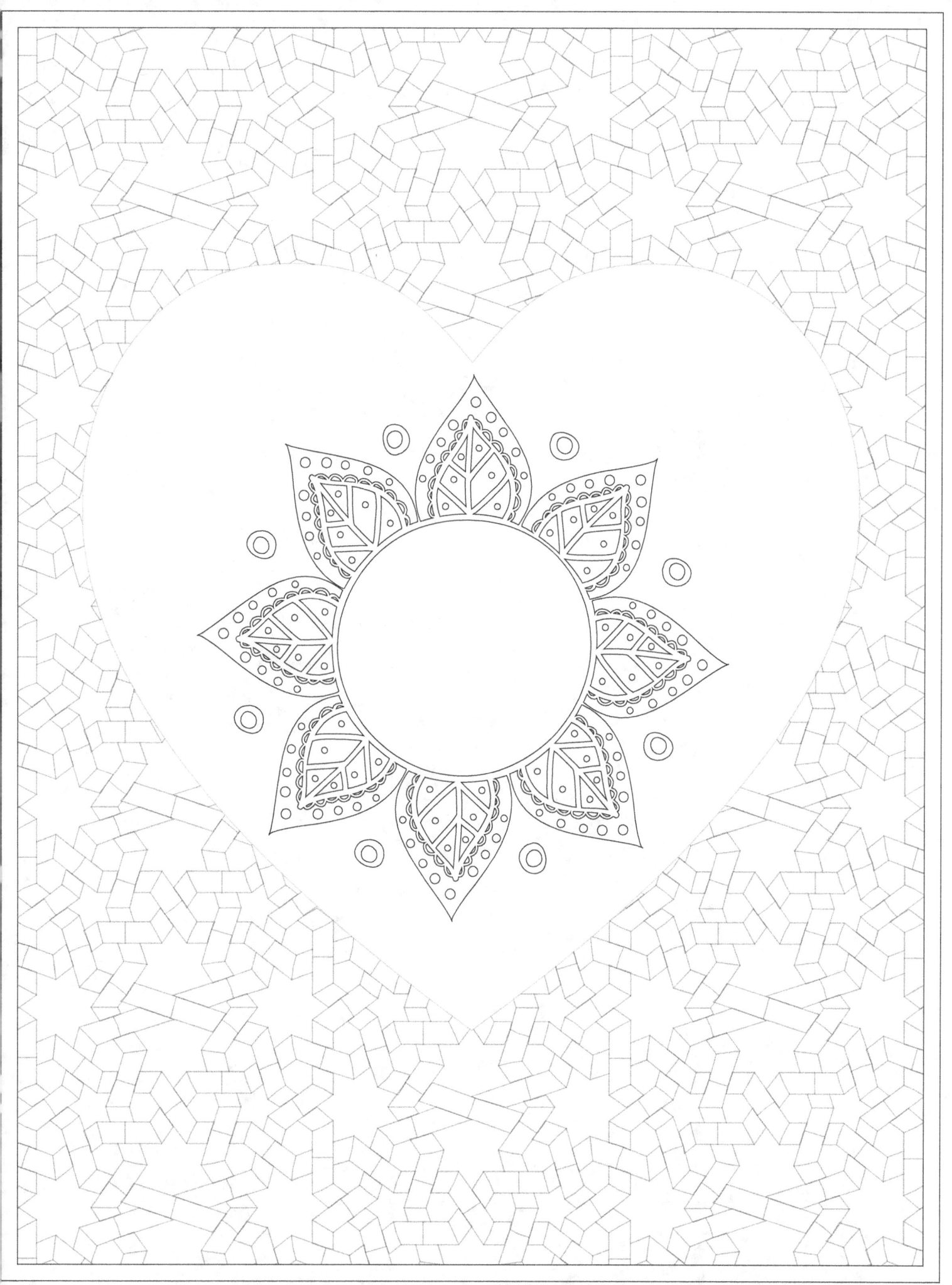

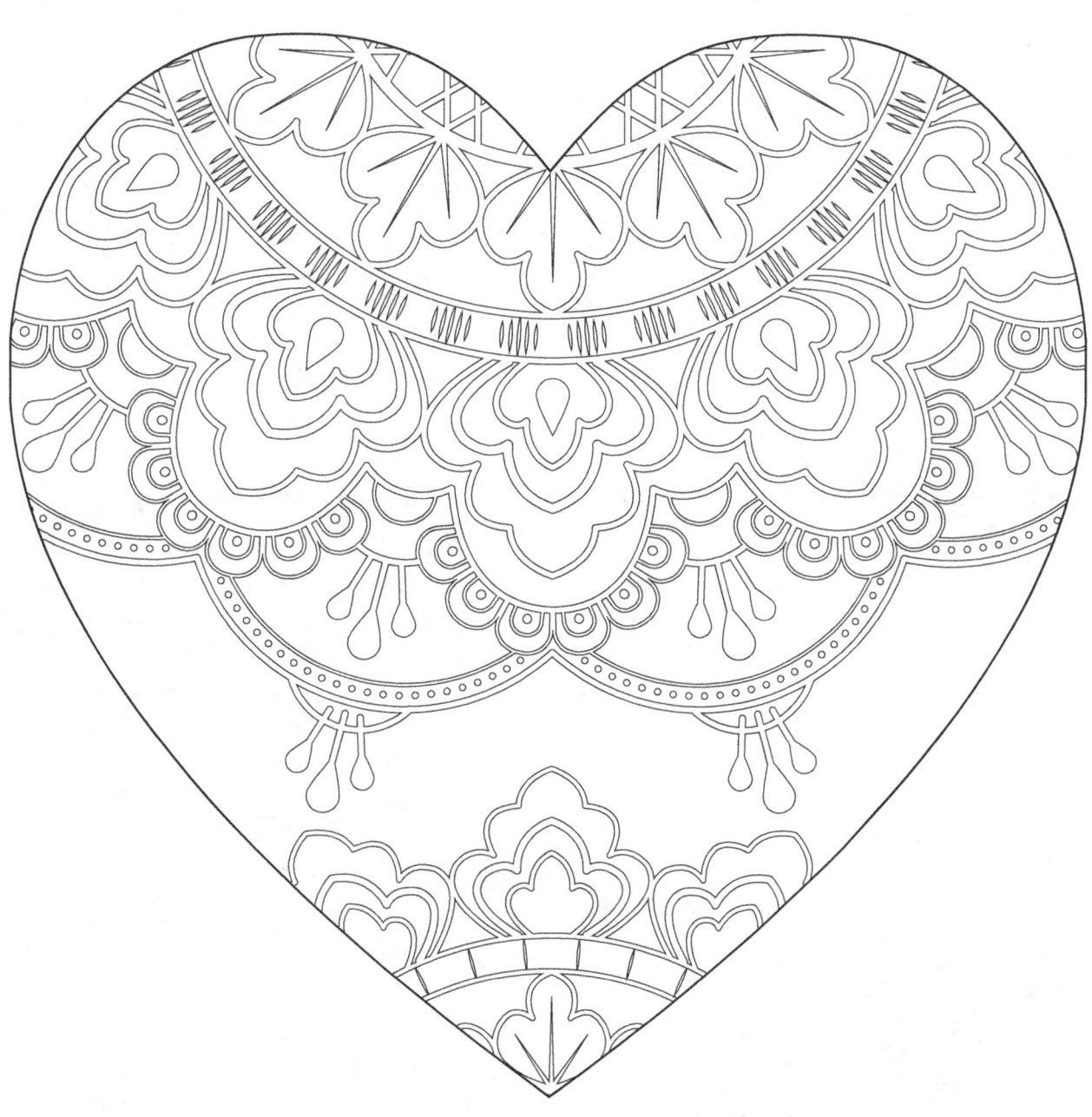

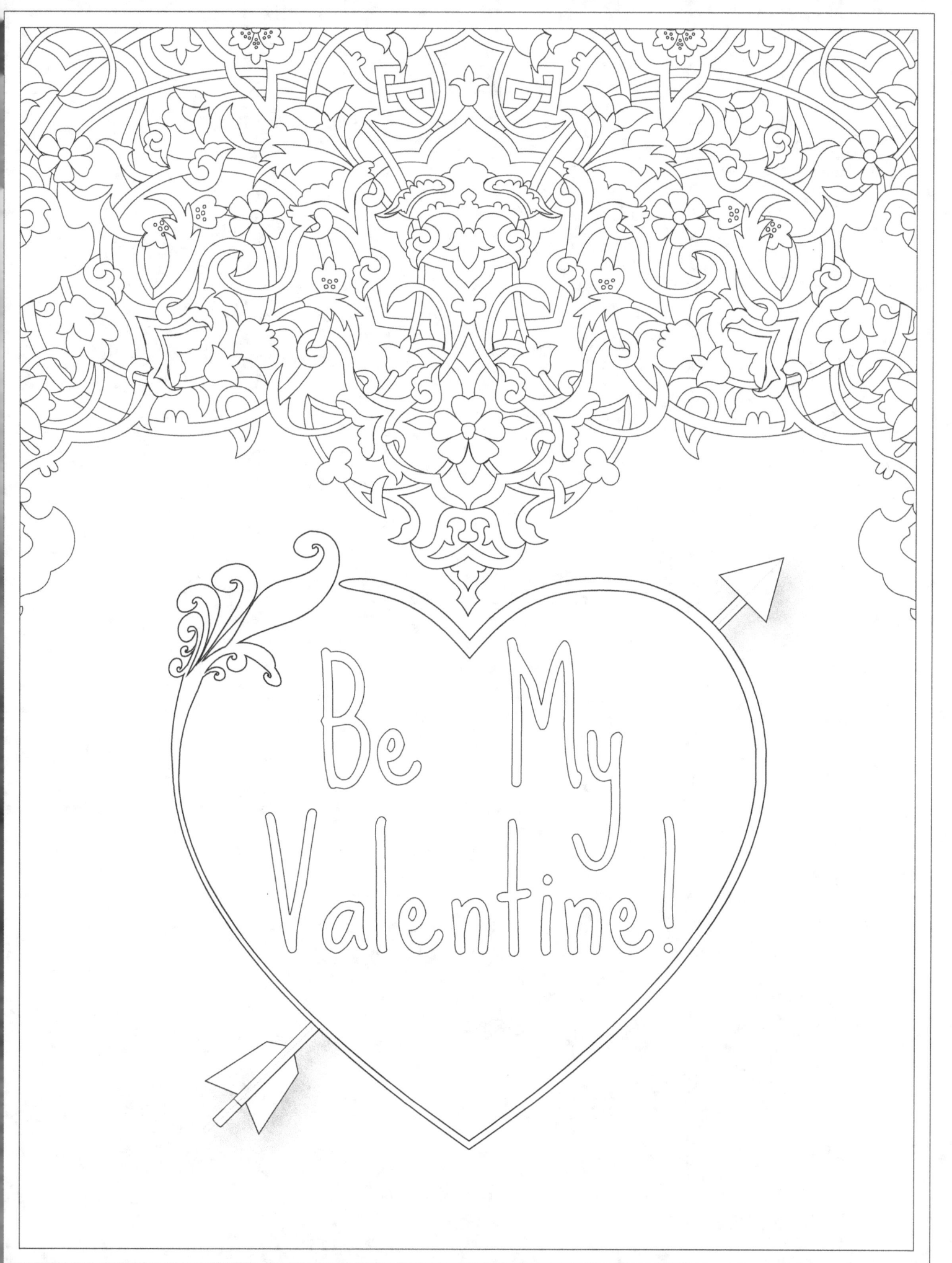

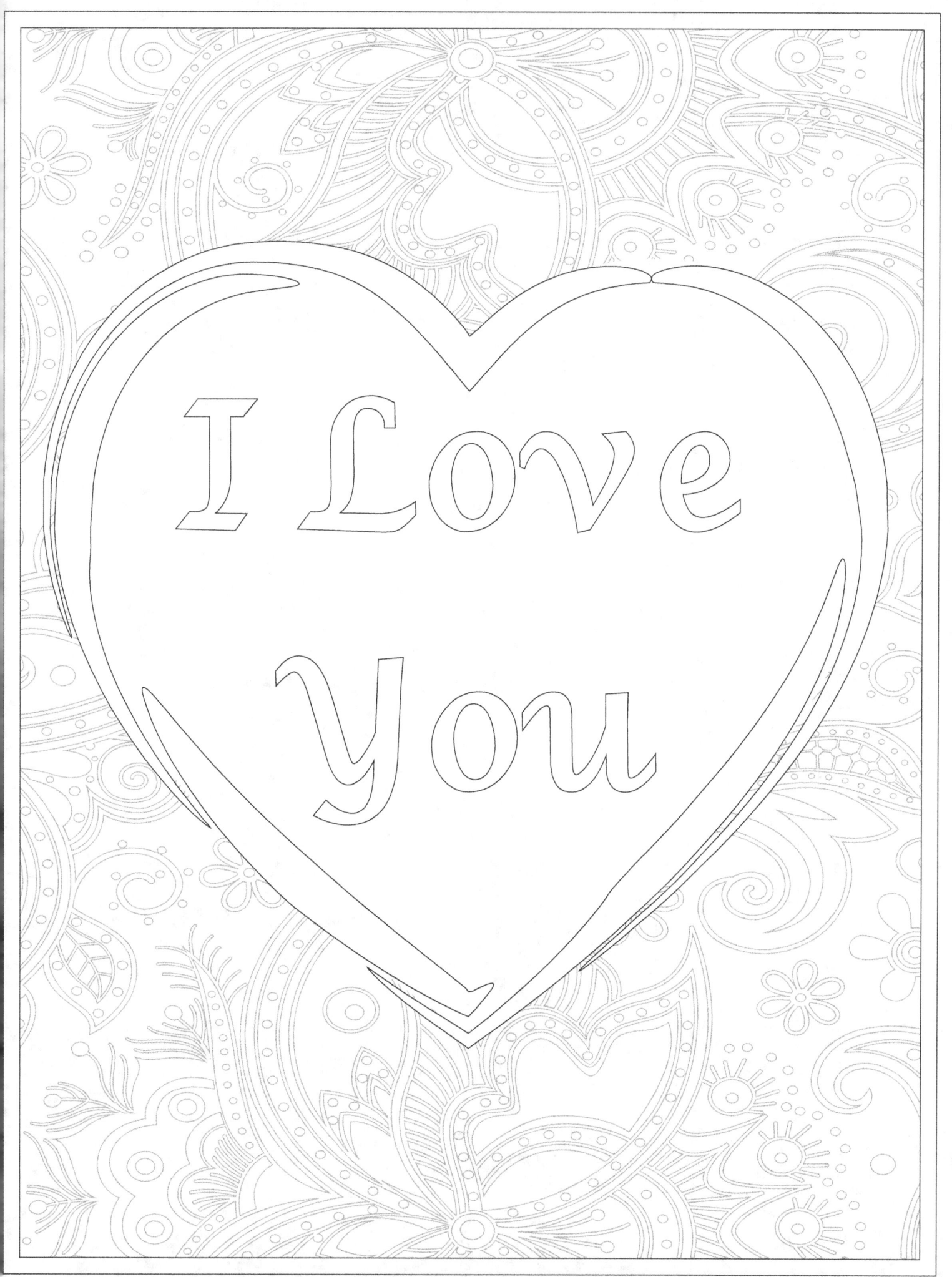

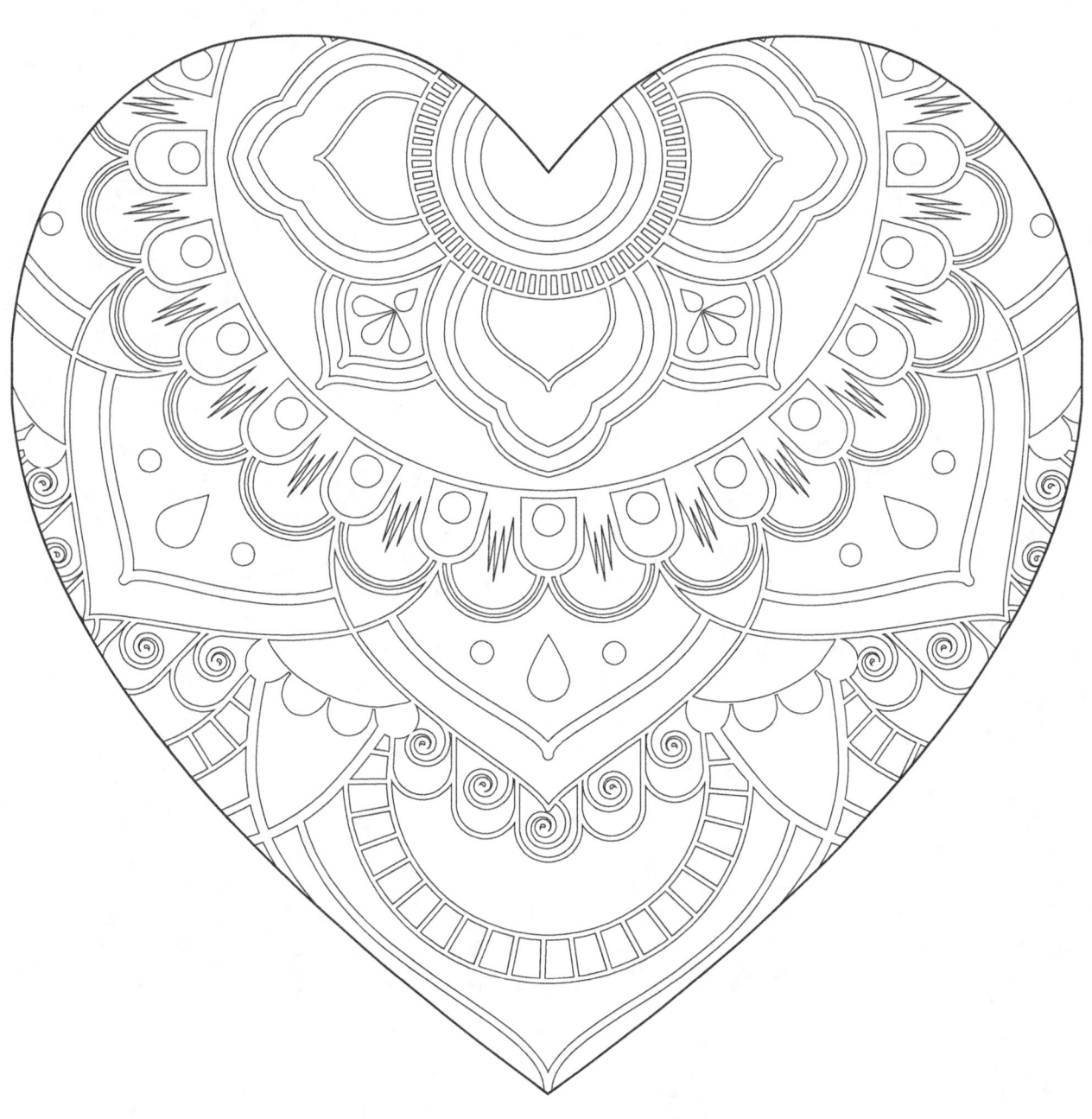

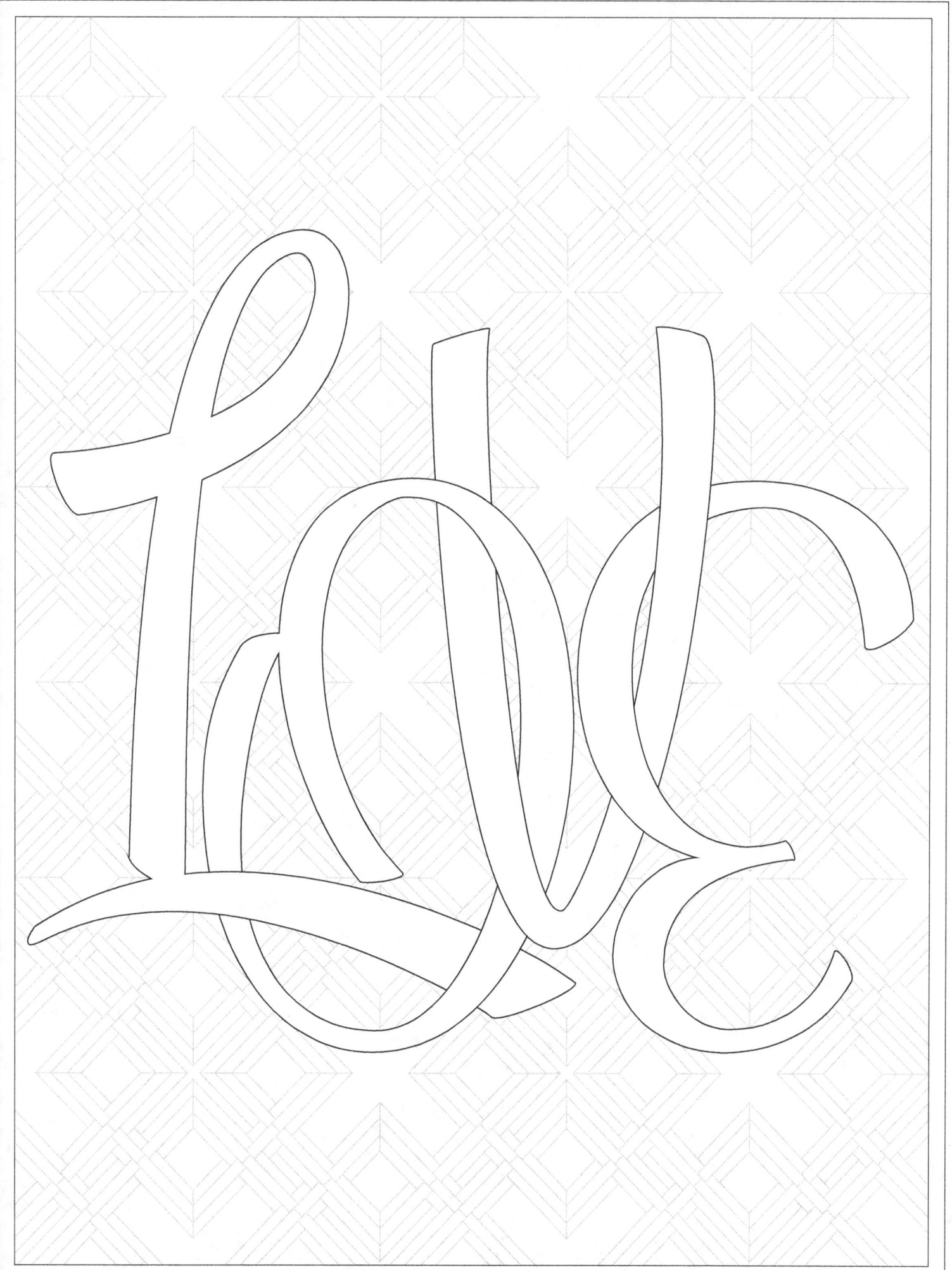

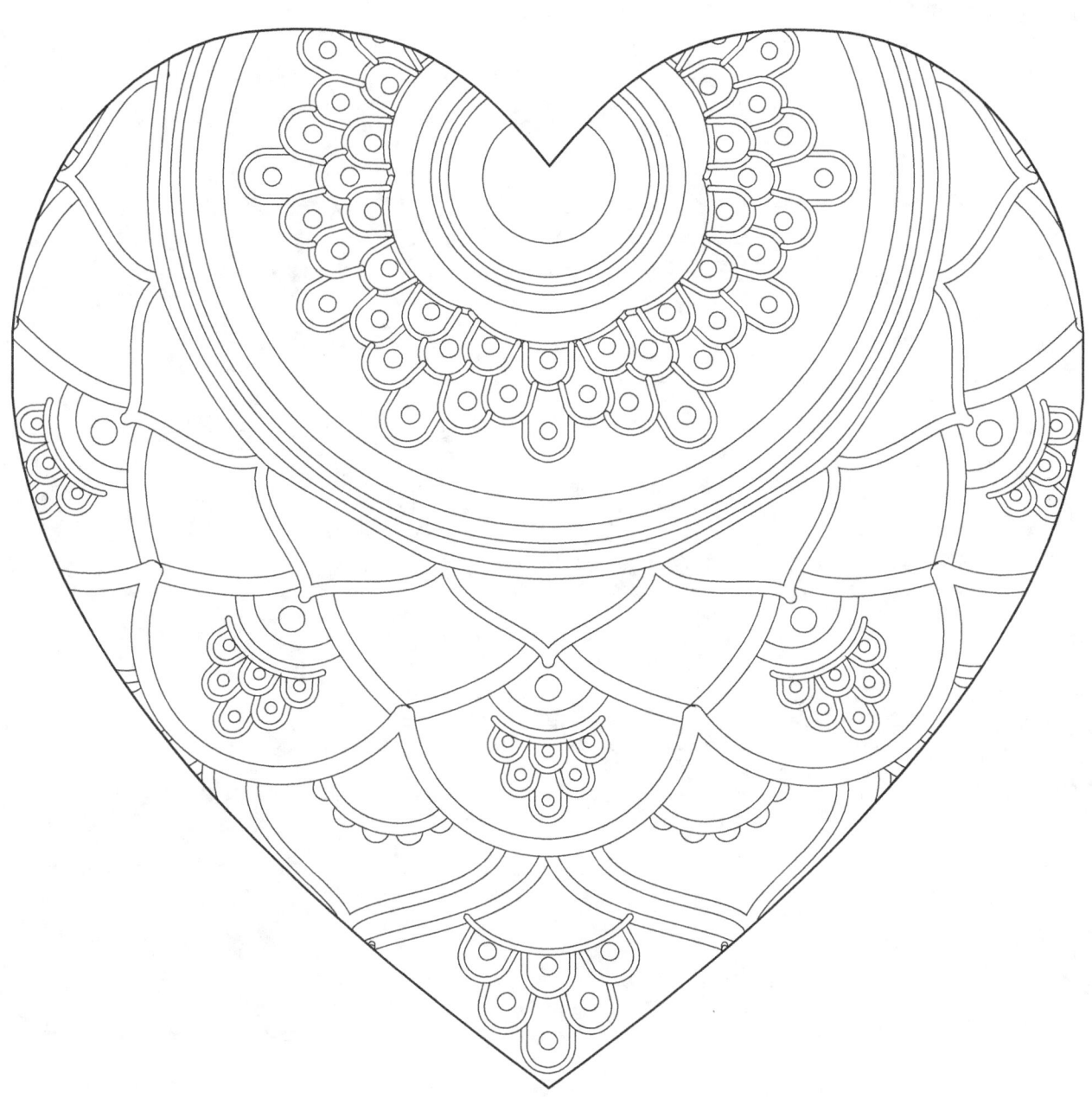

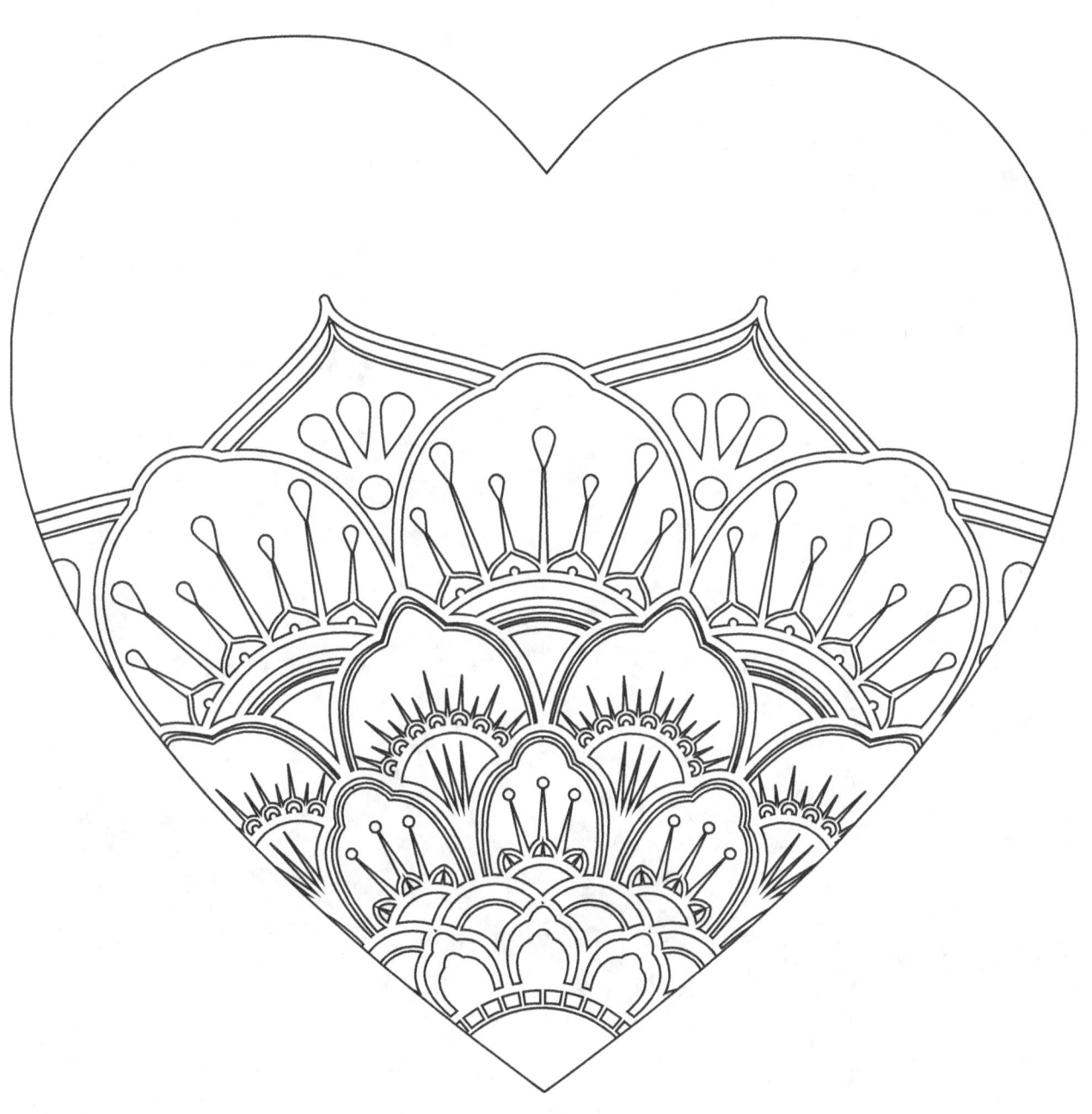

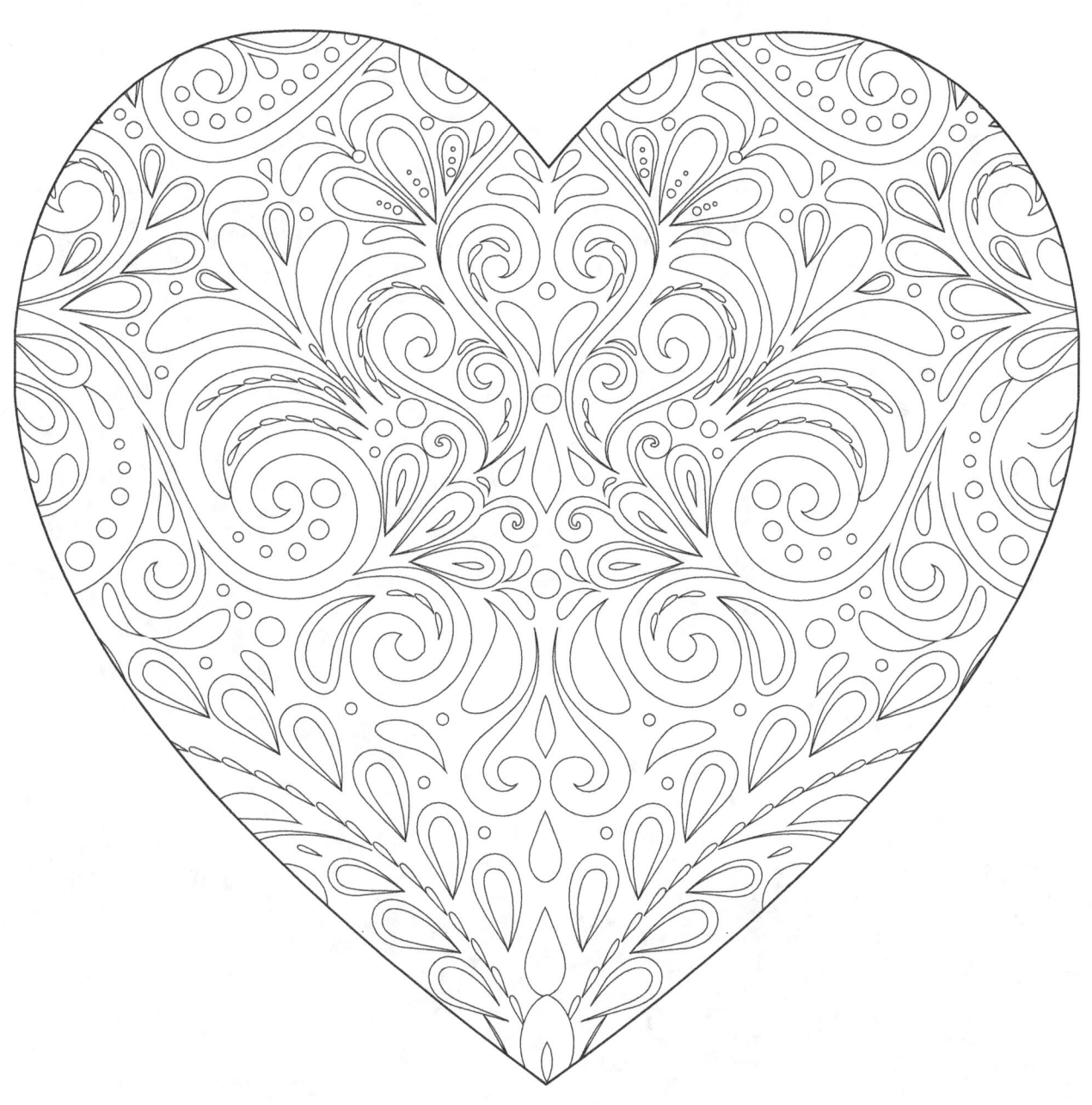